PARIS

First published in the United Kingdom in 2005 by
Thames & Hudson Ltd, 181A High Holborn, London WC1V 7QX

www.thamesandhudson.com

French texts translated by Frank Coffee,
Adele Kudish and Ricardo Bloch

British Library Cataloguing-in-Publication Data
A catalogue record for this book is available from the British Library

ISBN-13: 978-0-500-28559-6

ISBN-10: 0-500-28559-4

Printed and bound in China

Photographs by Max Derhy

PARIS

Introduction by François Baudot

Thames & Hudson

❝Paris is Babylon, the city of all temptations.❞

Christine Angot

Introduction

You drift in Venice, you meander in Rome, you wander in Madrid. In New York, you go from point A to point B. You often get lost in Tokyo. You always find your way in Marrakesh. In London, you catch a taxi; in Seville, a sunstroke. But only in Paris do you stroll. Sometimes this strolling lasts a lifetime. Paris is quite small for lovers. It's a city that you learn on foot. With the Seine as your guide, the Eiffel Tower and the Tower of Montparnasse, the Butte Montmartre and Bercy as cardinal points, you are not afraid of getting lost or being bored for very long.

The landscape changes constantly. There are benches
to stop for a while. Cafés to quench your thirst. And then
there are those booths—as in public convenience—
that see such diverse people pass through.

One of the best lit, best maintained, most logical cities
in the movement of its traffic, Paris, where all you have
to do is let your eyes and the soles of your shoes guide
you, is a reassuring city, except for Parisians who, from
time immemorial, seem haunted by its imminent
disappearance and tell you so whenever they have a
chance. No museum curator, no prison guard, no
palace concierge, no pecking hen has a sharper
eye than the Paris pedestrian spying the slightest
change that reveals a catastrophe. If a store closes, if
a newspaper kiosk is moved, if the direction of the
traffic is changed on a street, if the trees are trimmed
or the bus lane is made longer... a whole world

this epicenter has slid a little to the west, and stopped at the tip of the glass pyramid of the Grand Louvre. As a formidable manifestation of the power given by a kingly constitution to the five presidents of the Fifth Republic for over forty years, each of them has wished to leave his mark. François Mitterrand was a sphinx. He acted like one, redefining the entire tracing of the historic perspective which, from the colonnade of the Louvre, meets the place de la Concorde then lets the eye go free, past the Étoile, towards the open space of the Arche de La Défense... So many symbols! His predecessor, Valéry Giscard d'Estaing, who came from a liberal aristocratic family, preferred to create, instead of the old Gare d'Orsay, a museum dedicated to the 19th century. In fact, we owe him important systems of classification, the protection of sites that were not so much historic monuments as they were memorable places. A clever reader of Guy de Maupassant, who considered the Century of Lights as the height of good taste, this elegant graduate of the École Polytechnique put an end to the futuristic intentions of the contemporaries of his predecessor Georges Pompidou (who died in 1974). During his five years in office, the latter made significant transformations in the configuration of modern Paris, in order to turn towards a better future, even if it took authoritarian measures. Thus, old neighborhoods were remodeled, while the suburbs were refurbished through remedies whose radicalism, today, sometimes seems worse than the problems they were supposed to cure. The best of this vision, its substantial backbone, remains the Centre Pompidou. A large centrifuge that groups the most prestigious international modern art collections, a library, a center for industrial design, and an institute of in the center of the Hexagon, but it is its heart. The Louvre of Charles V, the exhumed foundations of his fortress prove it: even centuries ago, this was the place of power, which since has moved only a few hundred meters to the Palais de l'Élysée, familiarly baptized "the Castle." Capital of adultery, Paris remains strangely true to itself and to the rings that, like those of a tree, determine its successive limits, barks, and branches.

From the right to the left bank of the Seine, in the 12th century, the fortification built by Philippe Auguste, of which only a few vestiges remain above ground, still delimits the heart of the old Paris symbolically material-ized on the parvis of Notre-Dame by an inlaid rosette from which, sensibly, all the roads of France begin. One could say that since the construction done under the leadership of president Mitterrand in the '80s and '90s,

absence of undeveloped land, new expansion programs are becoming rare; though they are not missed
all that much because in thirty years, the builders have
failed to perfect an original formula that would recon-
cile the progress of modern times to the sensitivity of an
old city. In spite of its authority-induced bloodletting,
the banalization of the façades, and the destruction of
remarkable vestiges of the past, Haussmannian urban
planning appears today as the last successful, albeit
debatable, attempt to modernize a capital without
destroying it.

But let's return to history and geography. France was
the only country in Europe to take, very early on
during the second millennium, a compact and cohe-
rent shape that the monarchies constantly refined:
from Louis XI to the Second Empire, Paris is not exactly

hand with that of the small plants, factories, and workshops chased by the rise of real estate prices into the neighboring communities or even the suburbs. Given its small size, its intensive refurbishing, and the interests at stake, the notion of good and bad neighborhoods is less and less important for the younger generations. Living in Paris is now a privilege. Strolling in it is a pleasure. Leaving it is a sorrow; not only for the foreigners who have to go back home one day, but also for all those whose families grow faster than their incomes. For one, offices have largely invaded the buildings in Western Paris, traditionally expensive—less than 40,000 people live in the 8th arrondissement, against 225,000 jobs. On the other hand, the fashionable stores have gradually taken over, since the '80s, the heart of old Paris. Lavishly renovated, these old buildings are receiving fewer people and more wealth, while, in the live there with their offspring. The only solution was to receive the most deprived, the populations chased away from their continent by political turmoil or poverty, but whose power of adaptation, their solidarity, and remarkable capacity for hard work made them melt into these existing structures, which today, have transformed it into an attractive place, autonomous but open. This is one of the qualities of Paris, having known how to accept diverse identities, the most varied ethnic groups, the most improbable exiles, without transforming their natural groups into a ghetto. Each neighborhood is witness to great fluidity, as the stroller will discover. Its reality contradicts the very Parisian prejudices we had fun listing earlier.

There is no doubt that Paris still has slums, drug dealers, and unsanitary buildings. But their progressive disappearance in the last thirty years has gone hand in

Paris also has its neighborhoods, its exotic arrondissements, like Place Maubert, marked from the early '50s by Vietnamese immigration. In the Max-Dormoy neighborhood, between the Gare du Nord and the Gare de l'Est, trade is in the hands of the Chinese. There are a few totally Indian streets, full of saris and curries. But it is particularly the 13th arrondissement—working class in the past—which can be considered the Parisian "Chinatown" these days. The source of this unruly settlement is one of those urban planning failures of the '60s and '70s. A rundown habitat was to be replaced by a modern neighborhood, well equipped, designed for young couples with modest incomes but still wanting to live in the city. The architectonic choices were so mediocre, the high-rise buildings so similar to the H.L.M. (public housing projects) of the periphery, that the baby boomers simply refused to

Monceau slyly plunges towards the gloomy avenues of the 17th with, their large buildings and their small townhouses. Beyond the line of the inner beltway train, you stumble upon the old villages of Batignolles, Clichy, and Pont-Cardinet. Often called the "bad 17th," this section suffers, like a few others, from the railway's promiscuity. Bordering the tracks, the buildings still seem impregnated with the filthy coal dust of the old steam locomotives. And yet, two steps from Gare Saint-Lazare, the department stores have set up. A true 19th-century "bonheur des dames." Towards the Tuileries, the luxury stores begin, with place Vendôme and its jewelers. One could forget that they are in the 1st arrondissement, and Rue de la Paix in the 2nd, by the way they announce the elegance of Avenue Montaigne and the lofty air of the 8th.

symbols that have as many explanations as there are Parisians. The most famous, and also the most disparaged of all the arrondissements of Paris, remains the 16th (Passy, Auteuil, la Muette, Chaillot), a clan of prosperous bourgeois not sorry to be so. But the different arrondissements have other distinctions as well. The brave people of the 9th arrondissement who when, dignified, go up to Montmartre, don't like it very much when they are confused with their neighbors from the 18th, who, from Blanche to Barbès, engage in business of a more immoral nature. Belleville-Ménilmontant: the 20th, is a popular song with accordion accompaniment, while the 19th still radiates poverty between Avenue Jean-Jaurès and Boulevard Serrurier. Even the names sound poor, or worse, outmoded, like Place Stalingrad or Boulevard d'Indochine. The same, after the elegant Faubourg Saint-Honoré, the Plaine

In the beginning, there was Lutèce. An island whose boat would become its symbol, with a motto which is a whole philosophy: "Fluctuat nec mergitur" ("I float yet never sink"). How many Parisian celebrities could claim this modus vivendi? This center of the center of Paris, its starting point, the center of its 1st arrondissement, Lutèce still symbolically embodies all the temporal powers: that of justice with its Palais, of the police, with its headquarters, of the hospital with its Hôtel-Dieu. Even the Place Dauphine—in the beginning a group of working class apartment houses—was the result of an urban planning decision of Henri IV. In turn, the cathedral, the archdiocese, and its various services embody the spiritual power. This is the hard core from which the successive arrondissements spiral out. Their registration, from one to twenty, would seem somewhat dry, were it not pervaded by esoteric

loathes going to those suburbs, where suddenly he loses his way. Of course, he discovers that others can very well live there—but not him—oh no. Does this mean that the Parisian is a snob? Let's say that he is conditioned. Since the 19th century, the end of the Empire, the enemy or the barbarians have always come through the suburbs. It may be a Prussian or a Maugrabin, a communist or a bum… in any case they are not Parisians. In Paris, mistrust, like hospitality, has its limits. They both start and end at the gates of the capital. It's almost impossible to sneak in unnoticed. People from the rest of the country come up to Paris. Foreigners debark there. The ones who live there come home. But all of them, whoever they are, feel like they rise to it as one rises to power.

and a few archeologists. Four by four, they make up these twenty arrondissements, to which one could legitimately add two: residential Neuilly and its popular counterpart, the Saint-Ouen flea market. On one side, the Bois de Boulogne, on the other the second-hand shops of Clignancourt: air and dust, flowers growing, knickknacks languishing... well-beaten paths, these two areas for strolling would complete the picture of Paris if they did not belong to that poorly-defined area, rejected intra-muros: the periphery. By definition, it starts where Paris stops. Just one hundred meters further, everything has changed. The street signs, the stores, the way young people look in these suburbs is nothing like in the capital. The way people drive, their habits, even their words are different. For thirty years, an attempt has been made to organize the decentralization of France, but the Parisian still

Although it holds the promise of a great future in the concert of the new Europe, Paris is one of the smallest capital cities in size: 105 square kilometers at most. Berlin has 889 and London has 1579. It is surely also for this reason that one is so happy to stroll through it. From the center of La Cité, none of its points is farther than five or six kilometers on foot, hence the importance of a good cobbler. Like a baker or a butcher, there is always one every few blocks. People give each other the address like a family secret when singing the praises of their "quartier." These often have equivocal, sometimes mysterious names: Arsenal, Gros Caillou, Enfants Rouges, Gaillon, Roquette, Bonne-Nouvelle, Croule-Barbe, Javel, Mail, Plaisance, Épinettes, Grandes-Carrières, Goutte-d'Or, Amérique, Combat... so many stories! Created by an arbitrary division that delights the tax office, the land register,

Liberation. No, Paris did not burn. We can even say that it shines like the dome of the Chapelle des Invalides, like the Champs-Élysées at night, like the steeple of the Sainte-Chapelle at dawn…

Of course, these blunders have been constant, irreparable for centuries, like the bad moods of those who made them. Constantly changing skies, dog droppings, and above all this "hell of a life" give Parisians plenty of occasions to grumble about a city whose superiority they realize—by comparison—as soon as they are away from it. Because if few people are actually born in Paris, as soon as you are from Paris, you brag about it and you stay a Parisian forever. Wherever you go, because no city exports better. An authentic Parisian has to die before his neighbors, his intimates, discover that he was originally from Rochefort, Kiev, or Montevideo.

If Paris had anything to fear from modern times, it would be because of its imperious power to make hasty decisions on paper. Erasing the past, the transformation of the Seine front or of river bank roads, the refurbishing of the Porte d'Italie, of Les Halles or the Hauts de Belleville, proved to be, in the '40s, esthetic failures and human disasters. In fact, less so than in the rest of France, one does not schedule sunny tomorrows by decree. One does not decide on the joy of living in Paris... one comes to grips with it while walking around. From this point of view, in the second half of the 20th century, the city's beating heart escaped the worst. Contrary to many other European metropolises, neither the politicians, nor the wars, nor the urban planners, nor any of the good intentions, which indeed pave the hell of the streets, succeeded in committing the irreparable. "Is Paris burning?" Hitler asked the morning of its

collapses. People write letters. Merchants protest. Committees are formed. A few poets lament: "
Paris is changing! But nothing in my melancholy
Has budged! New palaces, scaffoldings, and blocks,
Old quarters, for me it all turns into allegory,
And my dear memories are heavier than rocks."

As a good citizen of his city, Charles Baudelaire hated "the movement that displaces the lines." But there is hardly a city that, since antiquity, has evolved with such harmony. It is as if, over its initial plan, each era, in successive layers, stretched its own tracing paper over it, redesigned or corrected a line, an outline, a section, until this superposition of transparencies makes up the Paris of today, whose slow but irresistible progression is like a spiraling snail's shell, formed by its twenty arrondissements.

music research. It is an ensemble full of contradictions, but Paris can only salute its success.

From the viewpoint of Lutecian topography, we must note the choice of the location of this artistic and cultural center. It is the first of the great Parisian architectural programs of the end of the 20th century that clearly turns to the east. Traditionally turned over to the less favored, this sector was developing much less quickly than the new quarters of the west with their greenery that seems to follow the trajectory of the sun. It was claimed that the winds that come from the Channel sent the smoke and miasma to the side where, traditionally, the disinherited lived. In the '60s, aware of the oval shape of the camp he had taken over, the General De Gaulle decided to push to the east to impart his capital with a new sense of balance. Today, Beaubourg, Bercy, the Parc de la Villette, its facilities and, more to the North, the Stade de France, embody the achievement of this desire for cohesion which, dare we say, closes the circle of Paris, delimiting its expansion for a very long time. Because with this last ring, made of concrete, of the outer beltway, the "Périphérique," the Parisian tree, as if it had been potted, no longer grows.

The fortifications of Charles V in the 14th century and those built by Louis XIII two hundred years later were meant to defend the capital. Yet, the gates of Saint-Martin, Saint-Denis, and others, today demolished, did not isolate the streets of their suburbs, like Passy, the village of Roule, Ville-l'Évêque, la Roquette, la Villette… so many small suburban towns, absorbed since. Between 1784 and 1787, at the time of the construction of the wall named after the Fermiers Généraux (the tax collectors of the time), with their toll barriers designed by architect Ledoux, from which only the Rotunda on the place Stalingrad remains, as well the one in the Parc Monceau, a pair of remarkable pavilions on Place Denfert-Rochereau, and two others at Nation... the idea was still surveillance.

Already too crowded in their city, on Sundays the Parisians would go for a stroll and a breath of fresh air under the ramparts to escape what was not yet called "pollution." They'd get a drink in one of the little bars that were opening up. These are our grand boulevards, where the great popular demonstrations still parade among the cafés and the theaters. Planted with trees in the 19th century, they are the link with those suburbs that were becoming neighborhoods, some elegant, others hectic. On the Left Bank, there are the students.

On the Right Bank, in Buttes-Chaumont, the workers. And by the hill of Chaillot, the nouveau riches.

It was Thiers who, in the early 1840s, determined the boundaries of the Paris, that is still very much the one of the "true Parisians," who, by successive cooptions, are not so different from the people of those days. Like them they would like "things to change," while keeping their habits. This line of defense punctuated by barracks and military forts corresponds pretty much to the current exterior boulevards, called of the marshals, because the marshals of the Empire were lodged there. They defended the Paris besieged by the Prussians in 1870, before they served as ramparts against the reds, in other words, the working-class suburbs. This is the eternal concern of the Parisian bourgeois who criticizes the rich but is afraid of those who are poorer than he is. We find them especially in this supposedly impossible to build strip that separates the "fortifications" from the surrounding agglomerations. Vacant lots, landfills, public gardens, a paradise for the homeless… Its magnitude is supposed to place the assailant in the open just long enough for the artillery to shoot him: this is what was called "the zone." The word stuck. The first shantytowns were born there, and so were the flea markets. Squalor embellished by popular songs and the nostalgia of these gypsies, chair menders, or horse fakers. It was there, in particular that, like the good strategist he was, De Gaulle decided to trace the final ring of the periphery. This time, the idea was no longer to protect Paris against invasions, but to facilitate its daily penetration by thousands of cars. Saturated before being finished, this wall surrounding Paris a few meters from the ground brings back the principle of medieval gates thanks to a ghost network of turn-off roads that often bear very old names: Arcueil, Choisy, Clichy, Saint-Denis, La Muette, Les Lilas, Le Pré-Saint-Gervais… Memories of royal hunting parties, hermitages, monasteries, or villages with country churches surrounded by their cemeteries. Any place that, for forty years, Paris would have absorbed by capillary action without this belt of roads that became its true chastity belt. Today there are no more red suburbs. Only tags, under the bad-smelling overpasses of the forbidding beltway. This is why Paris is so small, why it has preserved its integrity, and why it should also learn to grow in other ways than upward.

For thirty years, attempts have been made to decentralize France. That, which, for centuries, was strength, has become a handicap. Provincials like to praise the quality of their life. Parisians only see in it a mold in which they would be afraid to disappear. Because "their" city has a thousand aspects, at different times of the year, at every hour of the day. Less than a city-mosaic, it is a city-tapestry in which, under changing skies, multiple external contributions mix, giving it its true wealth. If in its shape Paris is affected by a fortress syndrome, and in their heads, the officials, who decide on its administration, often take themselves for Crusaders, no city besides New York is a more beautiful melting pot. Similar in this respect to the general movement of our art history, thousands of architects, artists, craftsmen, or simply amateurs (a beautiful profession), have built, woven, knitted, and injected throughout the centuries this great Western laboratory with a touch of the Orient. Robust fabrication, continuous, never limited to its own borders or its own memory.

From the temple in the Rue de la Victoire to the mosque on the Place du Puits-de-L'Ermite, from the obelisk of Luxor to the arenas of Lutèce, from César Ritz, a Swiss peasant who became a hotel keeper, to Coco Chanel, a girl from humble origins in Auvergne who became a fashion designer, from Jacob Offenbach, the son of a cantor in a Cologne synagogue who became chief of Parisian gaiety, to Pablo Picasso, the Catalan who, in 1940, was refused French citizenship, one can, since Lutèce days, be originally from Lisbon, Kiev, Saint-Pierre de Mézoargue, or Minguettes and feel perfectly at home in Paris. While so many others, who were born there, are not Parisians and they don't even know it. Though everyone sees it clearly: they will never be Parisians. It can't be explained. Or else, it would take centuries to explain it. It is they who hide behind every image of this collective work that has only one goal: to share the pleasure of being in Paris. Even when you are at the ends of the earth.

FRANÇOIS BAUDOT

The Zero Point is a milestone set on the parvis of Notre-Dame Cathedral, about 20 meters from its entrance. It serves to calculate the distance from Paris to other French cities, and it is said that if an individual sets foot on this plaque, he is certain to return to Paris.

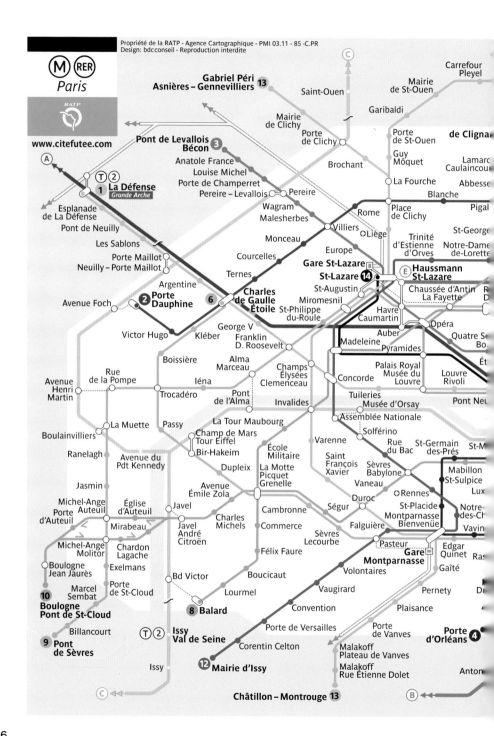

www.citefutee.com

36

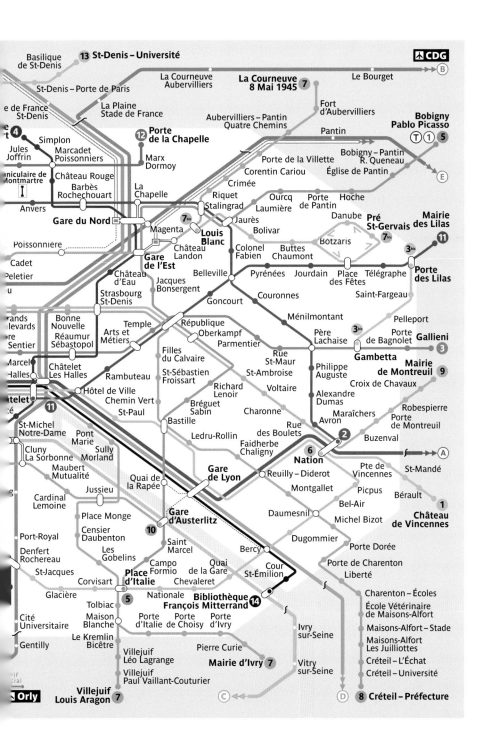

66 'I have often dreamed of writing a book about Paris that would be like a great stroll through it,' wrote Julien Green. Like an echo of this desire, this beautiful book is an invitation to walk around our neighborhoods, at the pace of its words and images, which reflect the 'soul' of this unique city, always on the move. 99

Bertrand Delanoë
Mayor of Paris

Advertising film, written and made by Jean-Paul Goude,
for Yves Saint Laurent's Paris perfume

" Paris is home to an interesting ethnic group that has its own way of talking, of thinking, and of acting. **"**

Claire Brétécher

66France, whether one likes it or not, has always defined itself by these few neighborhoods that go from the Esplanade des Invalides to the Boulevard Saint-Michel, and from the Place des Victoires to the Avenue de l'Observatoire.99

Marc Lambron

66What will become of Paris?
I think of it as I contemplate
in the fog the glorious buds
covering the trees along the
Seine like a light veil. Paris
has a beauty that disturbs me
by moments because I feel
that it is fragile, threatened.
Threatened above all by our
city planners.99
Julien Green

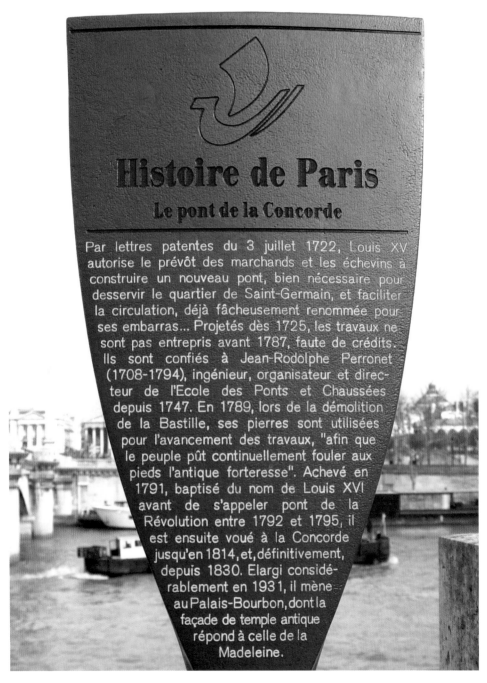

Histoire de Paris
Le pont de la Concorde

Par lettres patentes du 3 juillet 1722, Louis XV autorise le prévôt des marchands et les échevins à construire un nouveau pont, bien nécessaire pour desservir le quartier de Saint-Germain, et faciliter la circulation, déjà fâcheusement renommée pour ses embarras... Projetés dès 1725, les travaux ne sont pas entrepris avant 1787, faute de crédits. Ils sont confiés à Jean-Rodolphe Perronet (1708-1794), ingénieur, organisateur et directeur de l'Ecole des Ponts et Chaussées depuis 1747. En 1789, lors de la démolition de la Bastille, ses pierres sont utilisées pour l'avancement des travaux, "afin que le peuple pût continuellement fouler aux pieds l'antique forteresse". Achevé en 1791, baptisé du nom de Louis XVI avant de s'appeler pont de la Révolution entre 1792 et 1795, il est ensuite voué à la Concorde jusqu'en 1814, et, définitivement, depuis 1830. Elargi considérablement en 1931, il mène au Palais-Bourbon, dont la façade de temple antique répond à celle de la Madeleine.

"Whiffs of spring scattered through the air of Paris. Bareheaded in the sun. And here I am, strolling in Paris alone, holding arms with my fantasy, which smiles so broadly that it makes me, I think, smile to myself."

Jacques-Henri Lartigue

66 I walked for more than two hours, like in a trance, from Clichy to Opéra, coming back through République. I crossed a girl with endless legs in shiny skin-tight pants, she looked like a mermaid. I crossed some young guys sprawled on the sidewalk, with a small sign all misspelled, letting you know that they wouldn't mind some dough. I crossed children running ahead of their parents, others held back by the hand. That's normal, since I'd had one, the city had filled up with children. **99**

Virginie Despentes

66 Paris, I walk through you every day, and you pass through me with your faces, your cries, your tears, your laughter, your walks, your stories, your poems, your songs, your paintings. The photographer isn't a bad boy (you who pass on the Rue des Mauvais-Garçons); he stops, snaps and steals a moment which is available to anyone, and then he brings it back like a magician from a hat: in a postcard, a poster, a negative, a book. He steals what cannot be grasped; that which flees and fades from sight. The bird continues its flight after being photographed. The young man from the '50s has stopped here. The lovers are still under the weeping willow behind Notre-Dame. The lovers have changed, but love is always there, inviting us to share the moment. 99

Édouard Boubat

"The Parisian takes great care never to visit any monument. Ever. Except when its new. To be able to talk about it."

Alain Schifres

66 There are many ways
to walk around Paris. You can
set yourself precise destinations,
or just drift along. With a guide
book in hand, you can try
to systematically explore
a neighborhood, or else you can
just take the first bus that comes
along and ride it to the end of the
line, or you can try to go places
by taking a different route from
the one you normally take.
Or else you can devise a route
by deliberately imposing
arbritrary rules that will restrict
matters even more, such as,
for example, taking streets

whose names begin with
the same letter, or going
exclusively in alphabetical order,
or in some particular chronology.
In practice, these itineraries are
extremely difficult to work out.
During the course of one's walks,
with the aid of guide books
and maps, one can follow them
more or less in their entirety.
For the stroller who restricts
himself like that, Paris becomes
a giant labyrinth that during
the course of his peregrinations
gives him the feeling of having
left the beaten path. 99

Georges Perec

66 It's amazing the way people who have succeeded in Paris have of advising others to stay in the provinces! 99

Jules Renard

"Paris gave me life."

Paul Morand

Almanac of the addresses of the maidens of Paris, of every description and type, 1791, (excerpts).

" *Julie,* of the Ambigu-Comique, very saucy, never neutral about giving pleasure ; the prettiest eyes on earth, the smallpox left her somewhat marked but it didn't diminish her vigor. Two pounds. "

" *Dupré,* Rue de Richelieu, near the Library; formerly known in Grenoble as Ursuline; 25 years old, big, with a nice figure, white skin with lovely coloring, good teeth and firm and well-rounded endowments, small feet, every thing else in proportion ; she makes love like a nun, that is... passionately. 10 louis. "

" *Saintré,* Palais-Royal, very pretty brunette, charming curves, soft skin, remarkable rump, provocative demeanor ; she looks even better in the flesh and isn't the least bit expensive. 12 pounds for half the night. "

" *Garcins,* Rue du Théâtre-Français, charming. Everyone says she's malicious but her tongue proves to be softer than sharp. Price open to discussion. "

" *Carline,* Rue Chabanais, frisky to a fault, too well known to even talk about, we can't help but mention that she gives pleasure with extreme speed. 12 louis. "

Aragon

Il ne m'est
Paris
que d'Elsa

ANTHOLOGIE

Photographies de Jean Marquis

LAFFONT

66 This modern craze for the unusual has gone to a bizarre extreme in those covered galleries that are so numerous among the grand boulevards, and which are annoyingly called passages, as if no one were allowed to linger for more than a minute along these sunless corridors. **99**

Aragon

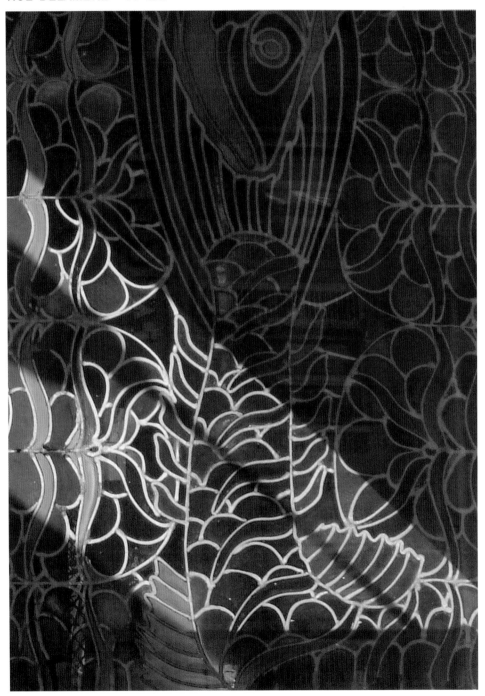

The pleasure of living in Paris

66 You have to wake up in the middle
of the night to appreciate what is unique
about Paris. The light, as it arrives, dawning
in the distant sky, is different. Paris awakes
at the crack of dawn and collects on the
sidewalk cafes as the coolness breaks
against the crusty croissants. And in the
skies above, the clouds drift about as if in
response to a soundless symphonic score;
they glide, they split apart and then suddenly
pile up in fleecy mounds farther off, then
stop as if a traffic cop had held up his hand.
And like an old couple with identical
habits, Parisians share the same sinusoidal
humors. The inhabitants of old Lutetia
are an unpredictable lot.
Wise men would have to be convened
to perform a close-up examination of
a Parisian. They would discover a strange
chemistry capable of transforming a city.
If they turn him on his back they will
of course find a label sewn on. Proper care

requires washing in hot water, but don't iron him too much, even if he's crumpled; one would also read that he is made of blends that could prove explosive. Such things as sweetness (just a little), gentleness (a bit more), causticity (now we're getting there), sweet foods (as much as he likes), spicy food, acidity (the harsh sound of traffic jams) and above all that amazing bitterness, that indispensable and disturbing ingredient found in elaborate recipes: the bitter chocolate in "hare à la royale."

One finds such a changeable mind precisely mimicked in the skies and their incessant variations. Who copies whom?

The clouds, or the people?

We should stretch out more often on park benches to better know ourselves.

The pleasure of living in Paris is that it never stops involving you in a certain chemistry, harrassing you, not seriously but just a little, annoying you, seducing you with its incessant simulacra.

Paris believes so much in life, that it is one of those rare cities on earth where when someone answers no, you rephrase the question, hoping to get a yes.
The pleasure of living in Paris is not just luke-warm croissants, self-centerdness, the smell of the morning papers, small independent bookstores, "cœur de pigeon" cherries, alleys, or bluish rooftops, it is also the cheeky way of looking people straight in the eye, or at the shape of their figure. It is also without doubt the reason that women here remain women late in life, and why men like to sit at cafes and watch them.
In Paris, people get dressed up to go to the market and stand in line to buy an old-fashioned baguette, or an avocado mousse served in a vodka glass. When you have them to dinner they talk with their mouth full about last night's dinner and about the next restaurant with haughty service they'll be going to.

The happiness of living in Paris is without doubt this complicated love (like the one for onself and for others) which forms this puzzling tight-knit solidarity, the way of returning a compliment, a flaky pastry, an argument; this grumpy side, never satisfied, wanting more, better.

Paris puts herself on a pedestal and believes that she is applauded, admired and envied, except that the rest of the world couldn't care less. But that just makes this dear old gal who talks to herself more endearing. Thick skinned, she can have a flare up while keeping her perpetual smile. **"**

François Simon

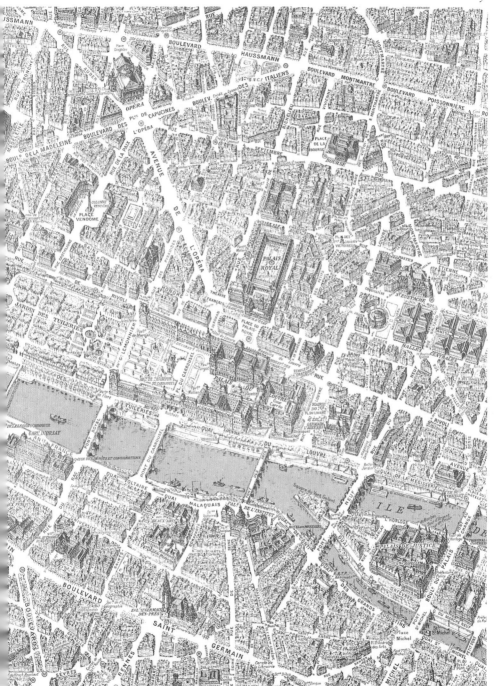

66There is something incredibly reassuring about metro stations. Even if above ground you are completely lost, below, you can always manage to find your way.**99**

Karen Elizabeth Gordon

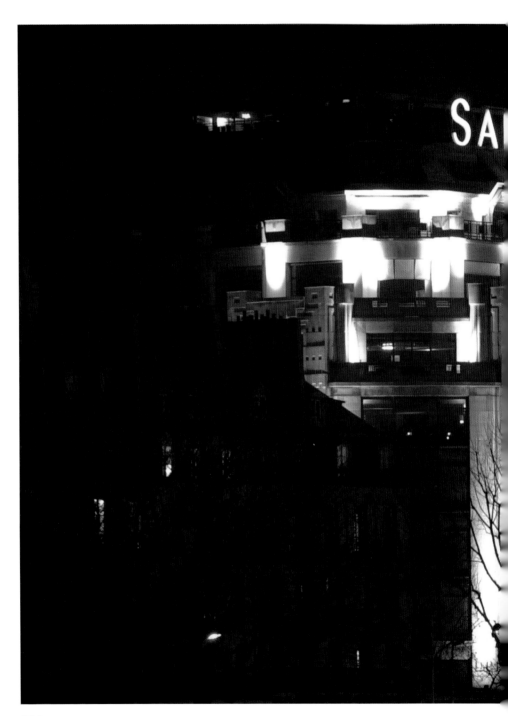

"The sky over Paris has its own laws that operate independently of the city below."

Paul Auster

"Je veux qu'on soit sincère, et qu'en Homme d'honneur, on ne lâche aucun mot qui ne parte du cœur"

Molière

Dimanche
6
Juin

19h30

Chapelle
St-Ephren

17 rue des Carmes   M°Maubert Mutuali
Entre le Bd St-Germain et le Panthéo

Concert
aux
Chandelles

Bach

Cello   Les Suites pour
Violoncelle

66 Paris is not a city, it is fifteen different towns! In Luxembourg Gardens one is with Gide, in Parc Monceau with Proust, and it is François Villon that one encounters in the Marais. I love the timeless feel of the gardens of the Palais-Royal, as well as its secret side.

I know a thousand passages with breathtaking workshops, and can imagine finding a new address every day. When crossing the Seine I repeat to myself: 'My God, how beautiful Paris is!' As if I were the first one to say it. Beside Tarascon, I don't know where else I could live! 99

Inès de la Fressange

66 Prodigious beauty of the Place du Theatre-Français, on foggy nights, the arcades and columns of the Palais-Royal. The Place with its lighted candelabras like lilies of the valley. 99

Jean Cocteau

The Palais-Royal is a small city within the city, surrounded by a Chinese wall, with buildings that overlap, that lean over, crush each other, protrude into each other and dig steep staircases and sordid passages that open onto Paris. At night, they lock the gates on these passages filled with black cats. They lock the gates of the Palais-Royal. They lock up the city inhabited by ghosts of the revolution.

Jean Cocteau

66 Paris is a city where one shows off, yet, paradoxically, it is a place where one can be both poor and rich at the same time. Contrary to other great capitals, in Paris one can get away without money or work, with just a little bit of boldness and style. This is a mixture that I find interesting. On the other hand, I avoid ghettos, the 16th arrondissement, and its opposite, the 18th, give me the jitters. I feel much more at ease amid old stones and souvenirs that remind me of my Right Bank neighborhoods.

I lived for 25 years in the Marais, before it became fashionable, and I realize today that if I had to move away from my birthplace, it would be to live while hold-ing my breath. Life is also a matter of breathing and this city is my oxygen. Far from it I choke. Also, I am proud to share my love for it, beyond its borders, through my work. The most striking being the Hôtel Costes, recognized internationally.

If I had a wish for the future, it would be that Parisians re-energize themselves and stop hiding behind their feeling of false superiority, and learn to open up to others, so that Paris will remain this luminous capital—this city that makes me live. 99

Jacques Garcia

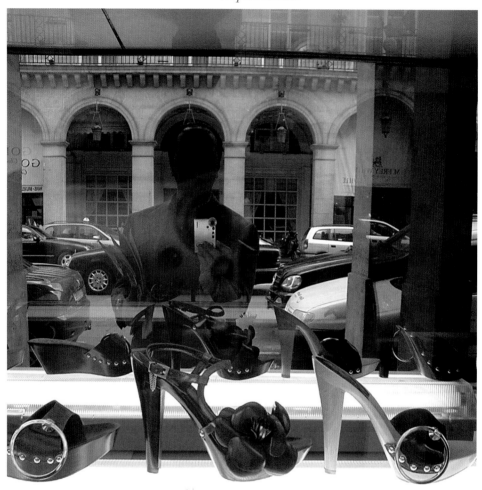

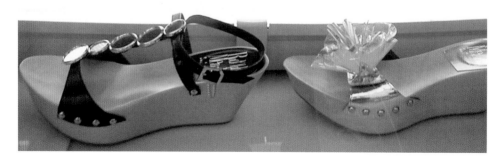

66The first arrondissement
of Paris is the smallest of all,
but it is the heart of it; it is
the kernel of the incomparable
fruit. It is at once the eye,
the belly and the past.99

Léon-Paul Fargue

66 Paris seems like a miracle to us. Especially tonight, with the banks of the Seine lit like you see only once in the world. In the water, upside down, you can see another city, more amazing than Saint-Tropez or Villefranche. Buildings whose open windows do not hide their rosy light, radiate piano music. Not a single radio: just pianos playing Chopin.

On Rue Montpensier, across from my house, the bakery already manages to smell of bread. The theatrical baker, with flour patches on his naked torso. His hat. His moving shadow. He is a true acrobat. In short, tonight, everything is beautiful."

Jean Cocteau

PLACE VENDÔME – 1st arr.

The windows opened onto the summery avenues. Paris was a string of dancing. Pirate parties in the streets, at the club on the Rue du Faubourg-Montmatre, the trees on the Boulevard Arago at sunrise, motorcycle rides to the Canal Saint-Martin, apartments in the 6th, the promenades to the Opera, Elvis Costello at the Olympia, balls, Lebanese dinners on Rue Jacob, the garden on Rue d'Ulm, the lights of June, the face you'd love to smack...

Marc Lambron

66 What I will never understand is why in Paris, they drink bad wine from large glasses, and good one from small ones. **99**

Jacques Offenbach

66 On my way to Rue Henner one day, passing through La Bruyere where I lived in my youth, at number 45, a house in which my grandparents lived in the first floor and we in the mezzanine (the ground floor only had a study which opened onto the courtyard and the trees off the Jardin Pleyel), I decided to overcome the anguish which usually makes me run in this street, closing my ears and my eyes. The door at number 45 was ajar, so I advanced under the archway.

I was looking, surprised, at the trees in the courtyard where, in summer, I shared my time between my bicycle and decorating puppets, when a suspicious concierge, poking her head out of an attic window that used to be condemned, asked me what I was doing there. As I answered that I had come to look at my childhood home, she said: 'You surprise me.' Leaving her window, she came through the vestibule to join me. She inspected me, did not allow herself to be convinced by any proof, practically chased me away, and slammed the door, raising with this noise, like a remote cannon, a wave of new memories.

After this failure, I figured I would walk the
street, from the Rue Blanche to number 45,
with my eyes closed, letting my right hand
glide on the buildings and streetlamps, as
I always did when I came home from school.
Since the experience did not yield much,
I realized that back then I was short and my
hand, which now was gliding higher, no
longer found the same nooks and crannies.
I started all over again. Because of a simple
difference in height, and by a phenomenon
similar to the rubbing of the needle on the
grooves of a gramophone record, I found the
music of remembrance. Everything came back
to me: my cape, the leather of my satchel, the
name of the schoolmate who accompanied
me, the names of our teachers, certain phrases
I had said, the sound of my grandfather's
voice, the smell of his beard, and of my sister
and my mother's fabrics."

Jean Cocteau

66 To breathe Paris conserves the soul.

Victor Hugo

66 To pass from a mint tea at the Mosque to the discreet addresses of the covered passages, which, when traversed from one to the next take one from the flavors of yesteryear and used books to old toys and antique lamps. Paris never ceases to surprise me. If there were more than 24 hours in a day, how wonderful it would be to meander, hunt for antiques and eat in neighborhoods that are truly miniature towns. 99

Alain Ducasse

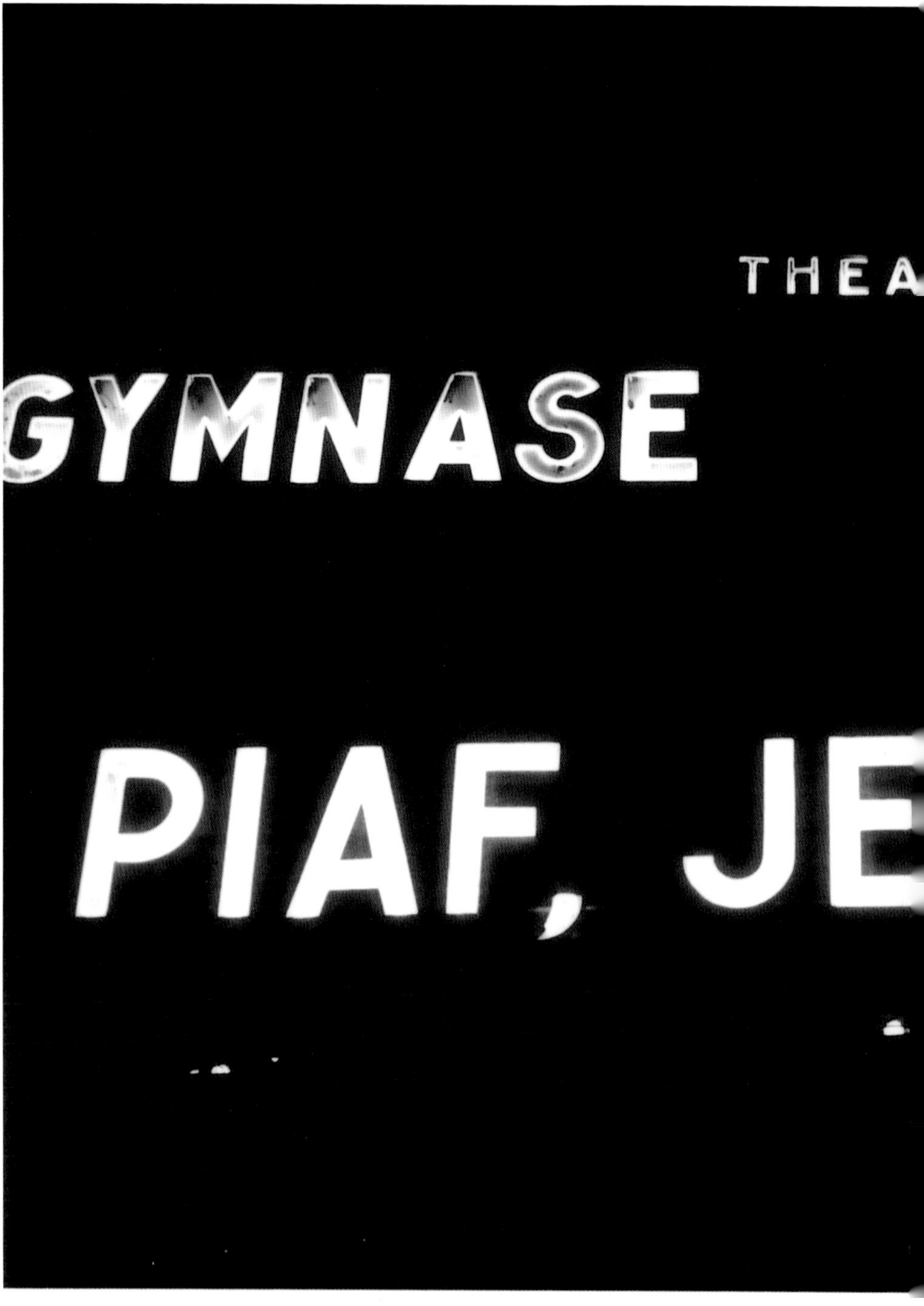
THEA
GYMNASE
PIAF, JE

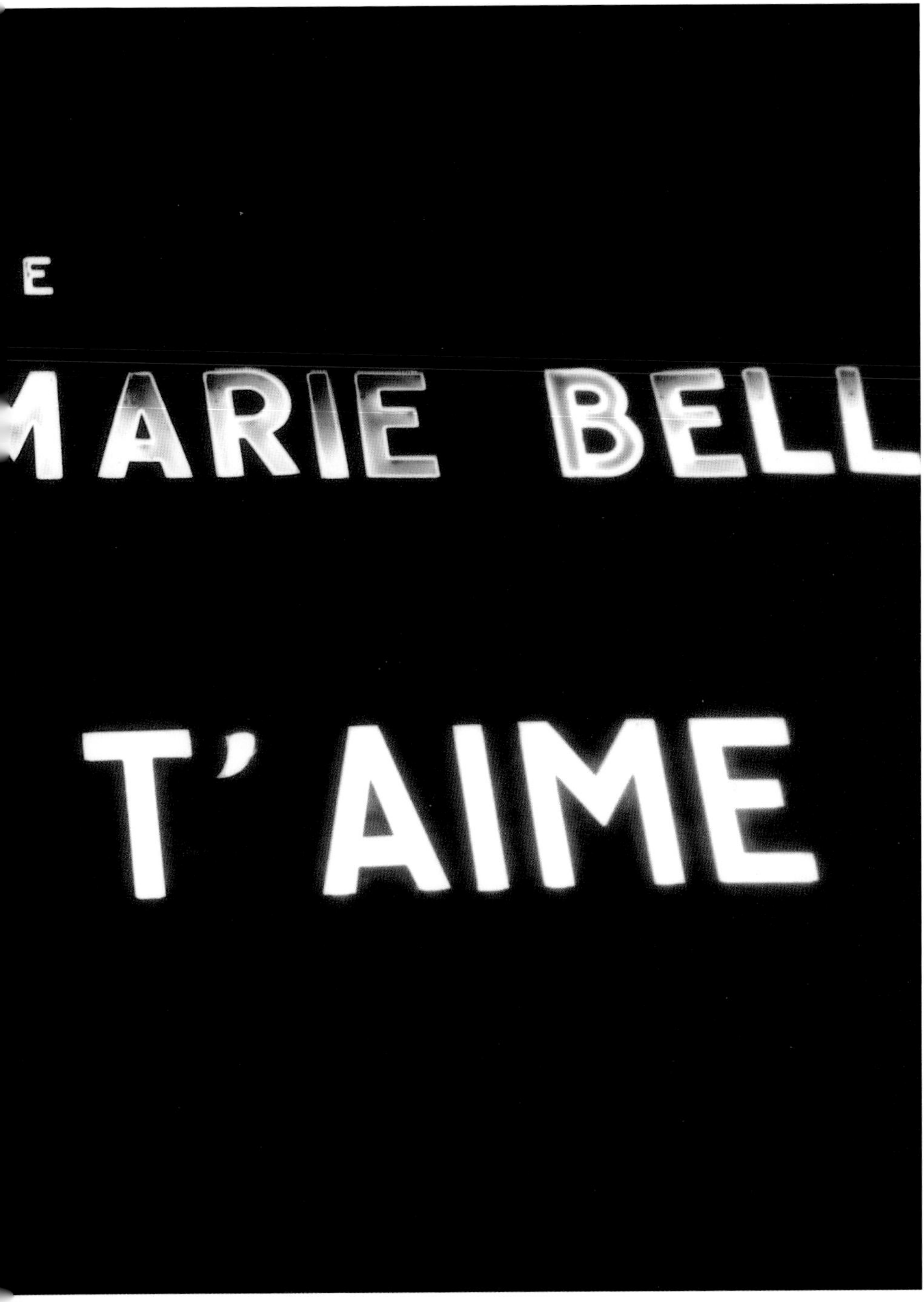
E
MARIE BELL
T' AIME

TÉLÉPHONE
TURBIGO - 77-48

316

66 What counts in Paris is the negative of the film that is being shot, the reverse of the décor. Twelve million inhabitants don't play a role, while, like in all democracies, a very small group writes the laws. Paris is severe, cruel, acid. Each person has the smile of the man who would gladly kill his neighbor, and who not being able to do so invites him to dinner. The dearly departed disappear like through a trap, without our even having time to realize it; each morning we check the obituaries and we cry for no one. One must approach Paris without preconceived notions. Having read Balzac and Zola, when I was fifteen I saw Paris as a cutthroat; an error as serious as believing in its smile, its good graces, its useless soil. Only time can give naturalization papers. By dint of not getting along with one's neighbor, one finishes by living intelligently with everyone. Wasn't it the great wise man of our literature, wasn't it the Victor Hugo of the 'Misérables' who said: 'Paris has another Paris under it.' In Paris blows are given under the belt, satirical songs are born in cellars, and new films, one must go down several floors below the ground to see them. The prize that will be given that same night to a novel, or better yet the reviews of a play, the opportunity

for a future loan, the trading price of a stock at the opening of the Market, a press campaign that comes out of nowhere, a ridiculous fashion that takes off at top speed, a good reputation reversed by that monster, Opinion, all of this goes through, at first, the underground telephone wires that borrow the voice of the sewers; the police listening in don't miss a word. Paris is a latent little civil war, the bursts come out of basement windows, the ball is grabbed on the rebound, the player, about to score, gets smacked to the ground. The most beautiful palaces are built with the hardest stones, Sisyphus's maybe, or from Scylla and Charybdis. Paris is a city of restlessness, like London is of lethargy; of invisible chatter, ground level gags, leg-trippings, savoir-faire, soufflés that can't wait, but fall as soon as they leave the oven.**"**

Paul Morand

"Paris is the world capital of cerebral flirting: one takes enormous care of what is said, but what is said is of no importance.**"**

Alain Schifres

343

" My longest voyage was the journey through the 4th arrondissement, the vital center of Paris, the plexus, with a stupefying diversity, good for an evocation of local exoticism. "

Jean-Paul Clébert

66 It is the arena of public life in Paris. What the Stock Exchange is for a mercantile people, the cafe is for the Frenchman. There, politics and the most recent shows are discussed. Every table has its group, and they talk so discreetly that the neighboring tables are never disturbed. 99

Donald Grant Mitchell

❝In his usual bakery shop, Bruno bought a long almond-filled roll, then went down to the banks of the Seine. The sounds from the loudspeakers of a Bateau-Mouche filled the air, reverberating off the walls of Notre-Dame. On the other side of the Seine, on the Quai des Tuileries, homosexuals walked around under the sun, talking in pairs or in small groups, sharing their napkins.**❞**

Michel Houellebecq

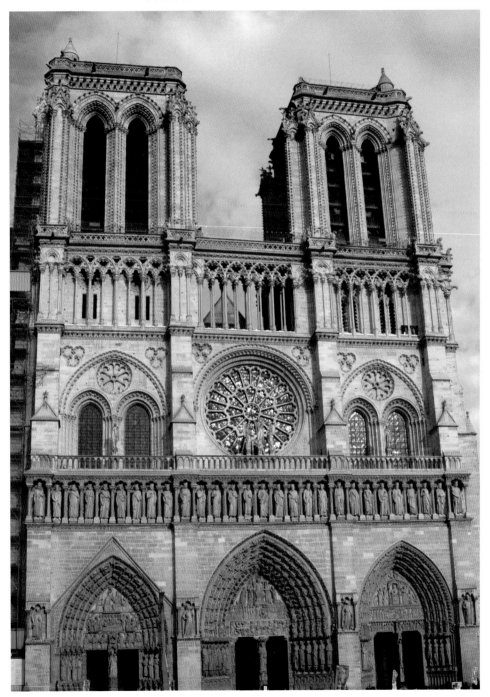

66Whenever I walk along the river I think of the time when the snow covered the statues of King Albert I of Belgium and Simón Bolívar, standing symetrically a hundred meters from each other. They, at least, haven't budged, each stiffly upon his mount and indifferent to the wake left by the barges in the grey water.99

Patrick Modiano

66 One is a Parisian just as one is witty or in good health—without being aware of it. The true Parisian doesn't love Paris, but cannot live anywhere else. The fish doesn't rejoice because it is in the water —but it will die if it isn't. The Parisian often curses Paris—but he never leaves it for long. **99**

Alphonse Karr

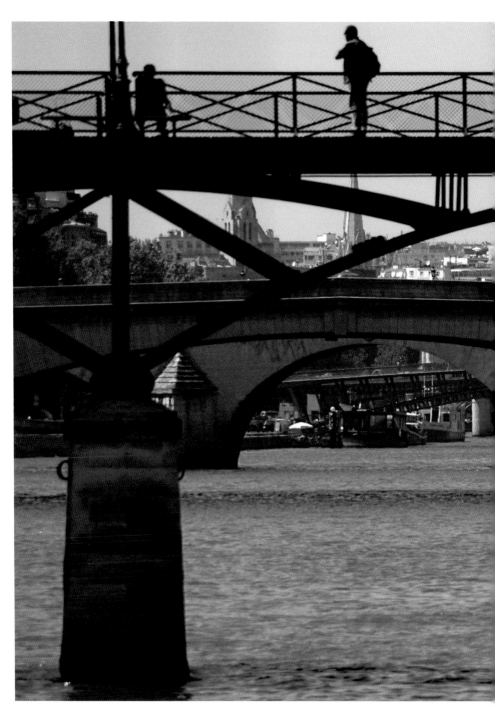

"There is a certain something in the air, in the look and in the sound of Paris, that cannot be found anywhere else."

George Sand

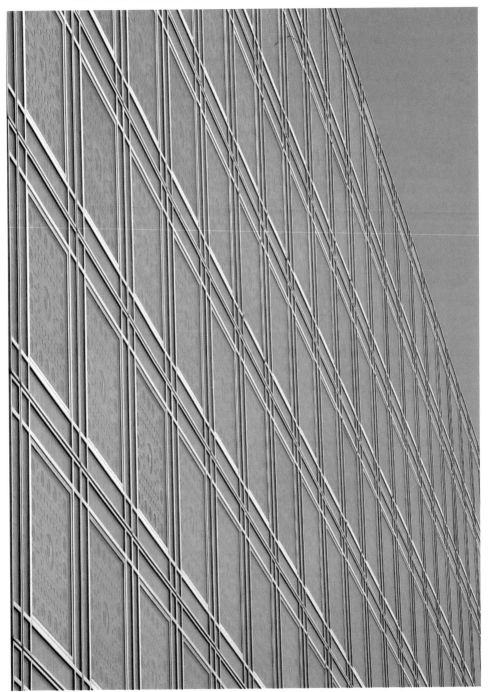

"The Jardin des Plantes is one of the prettiest sights in Paris during the day. When night and solitude reign over it, it becomes a place of enchantment. On one side the moving shadows of the animals call forth a strange world in the midst of the sleeping city, and on the other, the regular pattern of the flower beds bathed in moonlight releases all its charms without restraint."

André Hardellet

66Cluny Square manages to nearly not even exist. Its entrance is concealed. The tree-lined Boulevard Saint-Germain comes right up against its gates.

The garden can only be reached by a roundabout passage that discourages the casual intruder and only admits those willing to remove themselves from life, preparing them to keep as a tradition the ancient dream.

It is sure to remain peaceful.99

Jules Romain

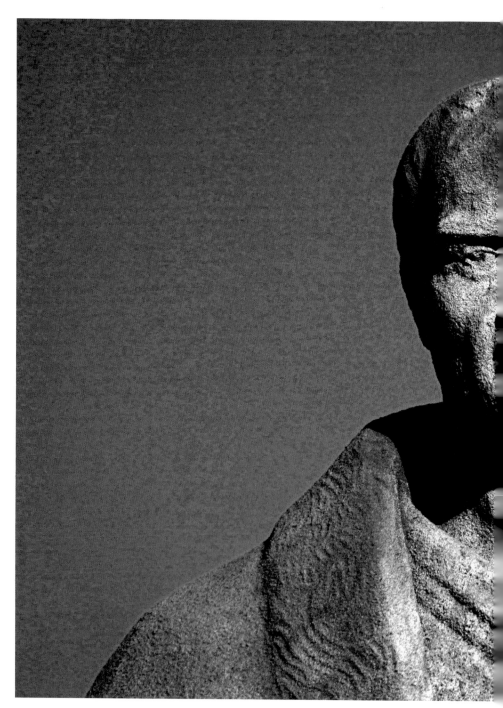

66Like any native Parisian, I am bored by the Champs . On certain days, however, that doesn't stop me from wanting to stretch out on the grass and breathe in the odor of the soil. But after a mere quarter hour, I'm ready to return to the shops and streets of the city.**99**

Julien Green

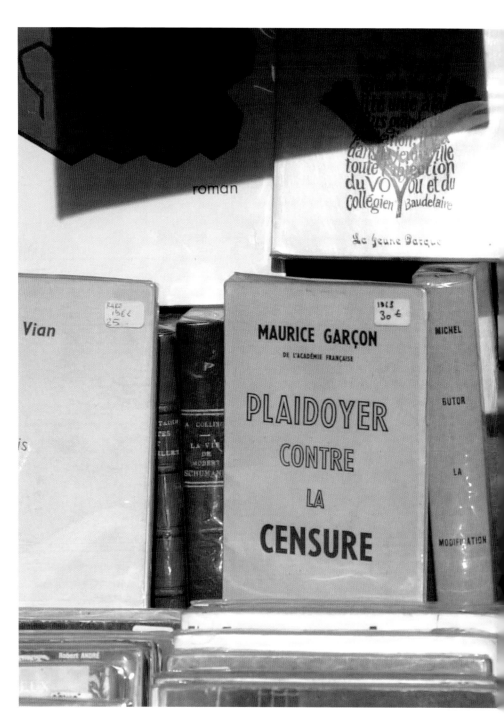

66The city is like a Japanese man in his scalding bath. My big convertible car takes me through the sunny, almost deserted streets of summertime Paris. The smell of tar on the melting road reminds me of other springs. And these memories form a big confused whole with the shape of love.99

Jacques-Henri Lartigue

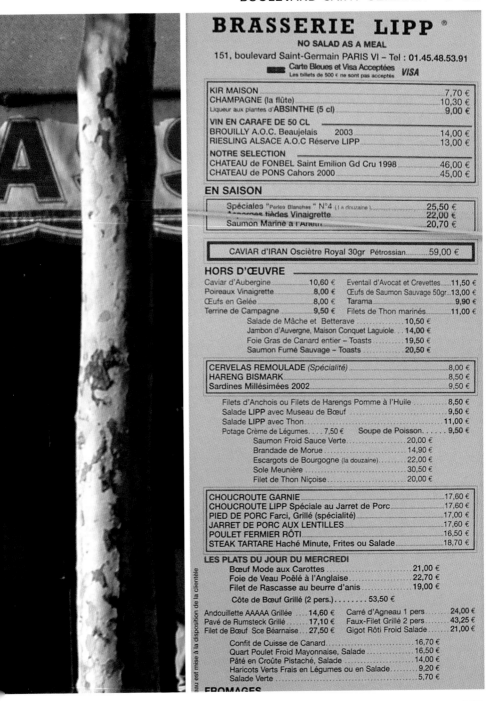

BRASSERIE LIPP ®

NO SALAD AS A MEAL

151, boulevard Saint-Germain PARIS VI – Tel : 01.45.48.53.91

Carte Bleues et Visa Acceptées **VISA**
Les billets de 500 € ne sont pas acceptés

KIR MAISON	7,70 €
CHAMPAGNE (la flûte)	10,30 €
Liqueur aux plantes d'ABSINTHE (5 cl)	9,00 €

VIN EN CARAFE DE 50 CL

BROUILLY A.O.C. Beaujelais 2003	14,00 €
RIESLING ALSACE A.O.C Réserve LIPP	13,00 €

NOTRE SELECTION

CHATEAU de FONBEL Saint Emilion Gd Cru 1998	46,00 €
CHATEAU de PONS Cahors 2000	45,00 €

EN SAISON

Spéciales "Perles Blanches" N°4 (1 à douzaine)	25,50 €
Asperges tièdes Vinaigrette	22,00 €
Saumon Mariné à l'Aneth	20,70 €

CAVIAR d'IRAN Osciètre Royal 30gr Pétrossian	59,00 €

HORS D'ŒUVRE

Caviar d'Aubergine	10,60 €	Eventail d'Avocat et Crevettes	11,50 €
Poireaux Vinaigrette	8,00 €	Œufs de Saumon Sauvage 50gr	13,00 €
Œufs en Gelée	8,00 €	Tarama	9,90 €
Terrine de Campagne	9,50 €	Filets de Thon marinés	11,00 €

Salade de Mâche et Betterave	10,50 €
Jambon d'Auvergne, Maison Conquet Laguiole	14,00 €
Foie Gras de Canard entier – Toasts	19,50 €
Saumon Fumé Sauvage – Toasts	20,50 €

CERVELAS REMOULADE *(Spécialité)*	8,00 €
HARENG BISMARK	8,50 €
Sardines Millésimées 2002	9,50 €

Filets d'Anchois ou Filets de Harengs Pomme à l'Huile	8,50 €
Salade LIPP avec Museau de Bœuf	9,50 €
Salade LIPP avec Thon	11,00 €
Potage Crème de Légumes.... 7,50 € Soupe de Poisson	9,50 €
Saumon Froid Sauce Verte	20,00 €
Brandade de Morue	14,90 €
Escargots de Bourgogne (la douzaine)	22,00 €
Sole Meunière	30,50 €
Filet de Thon Niçoise	20,00 €

CHOUCROUTE GARNIE	17,60 €
CHOUCROUTE LIPP Spéciale au Jarret de Porc	17,60 €
PIED DE PORC Farci, Grillé (spécialité)	17,00 €
JARRET DE PORC AUX LENTILLES	17,60 €
POULET FERMIER RÔTI	16,50 €
STEAK TARTARE Haché Minute, Frites ou Salade	18,70 €

LES PLATS DU JOUR DU MERCREDI

Bœuf Mode aux Carottes	21,00 €
Foie de Veau Poêlé à l'Anglaise	22,70 €
Filet de Rascasse au beurre d'anis	19,00 €
Côte de Bœuf Grillé (2 pers.)	53,50 €

Andouillette AAAAA Grillée	14,60 €	Carré d'Agneau 1 pers	24,00 €
Pavé de Rumsteck Grillé	17,10 €	Faux-Filet Grillé 2 pers	43,25 €
Filet de Bœuf Sce Béarnaise	27,50 €	Gigot Rôti Froid Salade	21,00 €

Confit de Cuisse de Canard	16,70 €
Quart Poulet Froid Mayonnaise, Salade	16,50 €
Pâté en Croûte Pistaché, Salade	14,00 €
Haricots Verts Frais en Légumes ou en Salade	9,20 €
Salade Verte	5,70 €

FROMAGES

eau est mise à la disposition de la clientèle

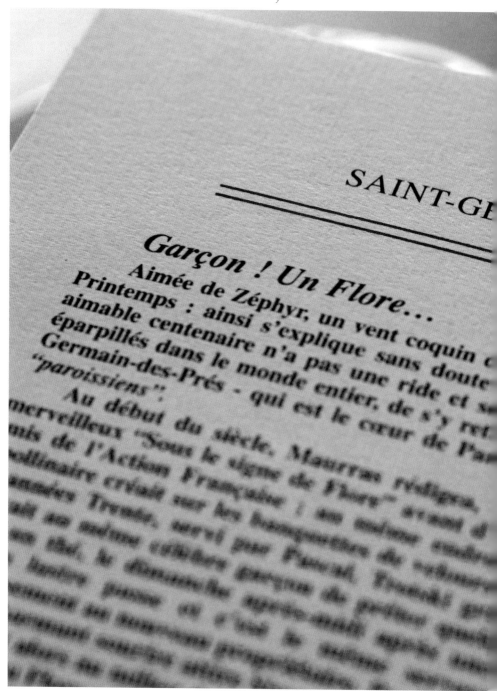

SAINT-GE

Garçon ! Un Flore...

Aimée de Zéphyr, un vent coquin d
Printemps : ainsi s'explique sans doute
aimable centenaire n'a pas une ride et s
éparpillés dans le monde entier, de s'y ret
Germain-des-Prés - qui est le cœur de Par
"*paroissiens*".

Au début du siècle, Maurras rédigea
merveilleux "Sous le signe de Flore" avant d
mis de l'Action Française ! au moins twelve
llinaire créait sur les banquettes du celèbre
mières Treize, servi par Pascal, l'inoubli
ait au même célèbre garçon du premier ge
Isadora, le dimanche après-midi aprè
landing pésent et c'est le
cemil les temporire perspectives ec

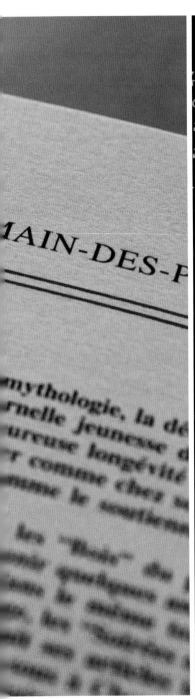

SAINT-GERMAIN-DES-PRÉS

❝ I was born in Neuilly. I began my secondary studies at the Avenue du Roule and finished them at the Lycée La Fontaine in the Porte d'Auteuil. I got married on the Boulervard Murat; and then I took a detour via the Avenue General Leclerc in the 14th arrodissement, before finally landing in Saint-Germain des Près. It is my quartier, my neighborhood, my theater, my permanent scene. I love its 'voyeur' aspects when sitting at the terrace of a cafe: the attentions of the passersby 'impressed' by the crowd, the unique-looking writers streaming by with a bag from *La Hune* or *L'Écume des Pages* bookstores, the faux intellectuals doing crossword puzzles at the Café de Flore while sipping a Suze and eating a croissant. The words, the objects, the air at Saint-Germain des Près are precious. We choose them, caress them. Nothing is banal. Sublime women crossing the street as if on a runway, others disguised, ridiculous, lost characters, like cutouts – and empty. The art galleries, antiquarians, and florists fill the air. The dresses in the window shops, scandalous or mysterious, 'eye candy,' surprised to find books at their feet. We know that all those philosophers, painters, and writers, gave Saint-Germain its tone and marked their spot: Beauvoir, Sartre, Romain Gary, Faulkner. They impregnated the air of the times with a poetic spirit, a living intelligence that is still tangible. ❞

Sonia Rykiel

66 This country
is that
of writers
of thinkers
of poets. **99**

Balzac

"In Paris, love is the child of novels."

Stendhal

466

RUE
DE GRENELLE
7ᵐᵉ Arrᵗ

RUE
BUFFON
(1707 - 1788)
NATURALISTE
5ᵉ Arrᵗ

RUE
DE
L'ESTRAPADE
5ᵉ Arrᵗ

RUE
DU BAC

RUE
DU
DRAGON
6ᵉ Arrᵗ

RUE
CHARLOT
FINANCIER QUI FIT BATIR
PLUSIEURS MAISONS
AU 17ᴱᴹᴱ SIÈCLE
3ᵉ Arrᵗ

RUE
DUCHEFDELAVILLE
ANCIEN PROPRIÉTAIRE DU TERRAIN
13ᵉ Arrᵗ

RUE
DE
VILLERSEXEL
7ᵉ Arrᵗ

RUE
LOUISE WEISS
1893 - 1983
JOURNALISTE ET ÉCRIVAIN - DÉPUTÉ AU PARLEMENT EUROPÉEN EN 1979
13ᵉ Arrᵗ

RUE
JEAN-BAPTISTE
PIGALLE
SCULPTEUR
1714 - 1785
9ᵉ Arrᵗ

RUE
D'ABOUKIR
2ᵉ Arrᵗ

RUE
DE
L'UNIVERSITÉ

RUE
DE LA
BOURSE
2ᵉ Arrᵗ

RUE DES
CANETTES
6ᵐᵉ ARRᵗ

RUE
COLBERT
(1619 - 1683)
MINISTRE DE LOUIS XIV
2ᵉ Arrᵗ

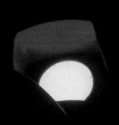

TAXIS

66 Clarification: a self-respecting Parisian woman on the Boulevard Saint-Germain never crosses on the white lines when the light is red. A self-respecting Parisian woman watches the flow of cars intently and dashes across, knowing full well she is taking a risk. To die for Paule Ka's shop window. That's exquisite. 99

Anna Gavalda

"The Paris we loved then Isn't the one we love now, and we approach without haste the one we will forget."

Raymond Queneau

RÉPUBLIQUE FRANÇAISE

A L'ATTENTION

DE MESDAMES ET MESSIEURS LES USAGERS

DU JARDIN DU LUXEMBOURG

Le Sénat met à votre disposition un grand nombre de chaises, de fauteuils et de bancs. Pour autant, la quantité de ceux-ci ne peut satisfaire chaque visiteur, notamment les jours de grande affluence.

Pour permettre au maximum des visiteurs de se reposer, il est recommandé à chacun de *n'utiliser qu'une seule chaise ou un seul fauteuil.*

66The Paris of our childhood, where our early photos show us a Place de la Concorde with five fiacres and 18 passers-by. The Paris of 1900 smelled of absinthe; it was still the setting for the 'Education sentimentale' where Frédéric Moreau felt lost, that summer, in front of the empty cafes. Sacred memories haunt me at every corner; for example, at 5 Rue de l'École-de-Médecine, in the house where Sarah Bernhardt was born, I had a studio on the top floor of the School of Decorative Arts, run by my father; my windows looked out on the refectory of the Franciscan friars with its 14th-century nave, which is today the Dupuytren Museum. In the courtyard, under an 18th century cupola, David once taught drawing; in the depths of the basement, our cellars went down to a Jewish cemetery from the time of Phillip the Handsome; digging further, one came upon the ruins of a Roman palace, without doubt an annex of the Roman baths, beneath the Boulevard Saint Michel.**"**

Paul Morand

"The steel skeleton shivers in the cold wind, awaiting the hour when its electric lights will sparkle like champagne."

Henry Miller

66 The Seine is rising, yellowish-green, heavy and majestic, it is flooding both banks. The arches of the bridges seem to bow down before it. It is menacing, proud. I think it's magnificent in moments such as these, when it is full of rage, a sovereign rage. The dark grey sky makes of Paris a white city. Notre-Dame, splendor of youth. 99

Julien Green

> 66In 1861, Paris renamed the Avenue d'Eylau for its most famous resident, whose friends thenceforth addressed their letters: 'To M. Victor Hugo, in his own avenue, Paris.'99

Jean-Paul Caracalla

586

587

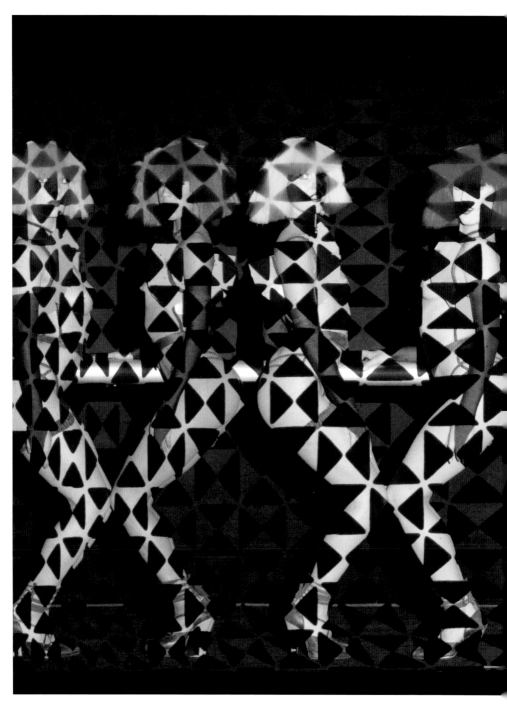

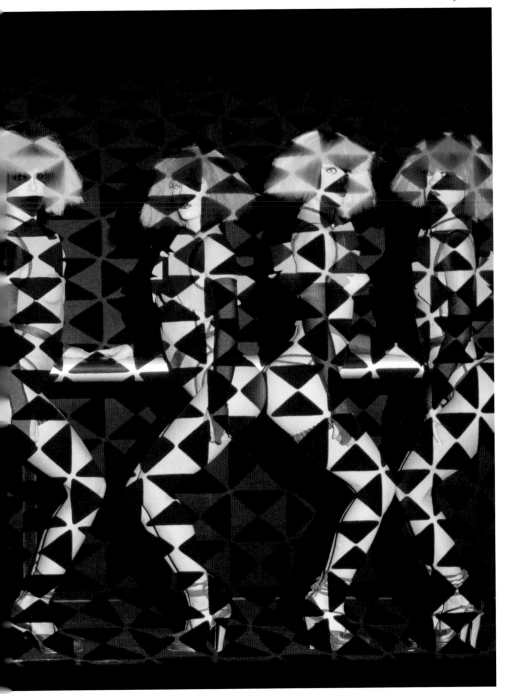

66 Over time I have learned how to tell if a person has become integrated to Parisian life: by his attitude toward pigeons. Most foreigners adore them; they see them as beautiful and picturesque birds that fly around the squares and sleep leaning against each other on window sills or roofs, pecking corn from the nervous outstretched hands of children in public gardens. On the other hand, Parisians detest them. **99**

Juan Carlos Botero

"Oh, to stroll in Paris! Strolling is a science, the eye's gastronomy. To go for a walk is to vegetate. To stroll is to live."

Balzac

"Nostalgic stroll through Paris. Rostand's haunts make you think of destiny. Parks, the Eiffel Tower, actresses, bakers' wives, haute-couture: that's France, madam."

Marc Lambron

666

66To live Paris is to kiss your lover long and deep on some bridge or other. It is to arrive soaking at a gleaming square and search in agony for the face that never apears. To live Paris is to rush into the metro fearful of being late for an adulterous tryst, or to take refuge with freezing hands in some out-of-the-way cafe. The cafe, a place for lovers. Because there is a Parisian way of loving, and whoever falls in love in Paris cannot love any other way.99

Zoé Valdés

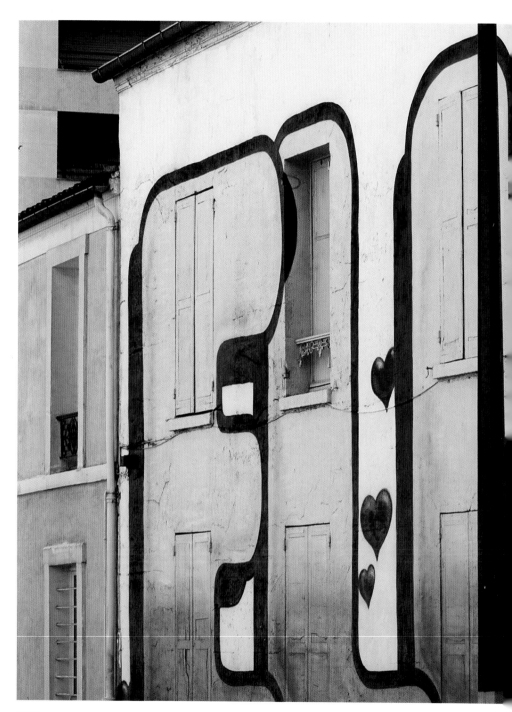

PARC GEORGES-BRASSENS – 15th arr.

❝I will spend the rest of my life Watching the Seine flow by... It is a poem in Paris.❞

Blaise Cendrars

66 Mistrust is the rule in Paris. It oozes from the pavement, it rises out of each metro station and from the sewer grates, it exudes from each box at the Opéra. In Paris, what is visible counts less than what is hidden. The salons that are chronicled in the newspapers—who ignore what those in the know know full well—are but public gatherings without importance. The names of the smart set on opening nights impress only provincial gossip columnists. When a restaurant achieves renown, or rises to three stars, it is a sign that it has been six months since they were abandoned by the real connoisseurs. 99

Paul Morand

TOUR MONTPARNASSE – 14th arr.

66 When I entered Léon-Paul's
small apartment on the Boulevard
Montparnasse, where many of
the greatest artists of our time, and
many a regal socialite, had left
behind a sort of luxurious fragrance,
I had the fleeting sensation that fate
had led me into the world to which
I had always wanted to belong
without even knowing it existed
or that it was so perfect, and that
all I had to do to attain it was to take
the metro and get off at Duroc. 99

Jean Dutourd

CUBANA Café

RESTAURANT
Le Parc aux Cerfs

≡BAR≡

Le Select

CINEMA
EUROPA
PANTHÉON

Le Dome

La Coupole

Rosebud
bar

le bar à huîtres

ROYAL
LUXEMBOURG

Restaurant

NICOLAS

La Closerie
RESTAURANT BAR
des Lilas

JAZZ BAR

LE PETIT JOURNAL

LE PETIT
JOURNAL

**"It is Paname that made me,
And Paris that celebrates me!
I have it in my skin,
I'm a darling of Paname's...
You become queen for a day,
Under the lights of Belleville,
And remain so through the nights...
And then... for a whole life!
Paris à gogo
Paris my star of the planet
Paris-Paris
It is my whole energy.
Paris/Paname
My life, my soul."**

Régine

66 There is never any end to Paris, and the memory of each person who has lived in it differs from that of any other. We always returned to it no matter who we were or how it was changed or with what difficulties, or ease, it could be reached. Paris was always worth it and you received return for whatever you brought to it. But this is how Paris was in the early days when we were very poor and very happy.

Ernest Hemingway 99

740

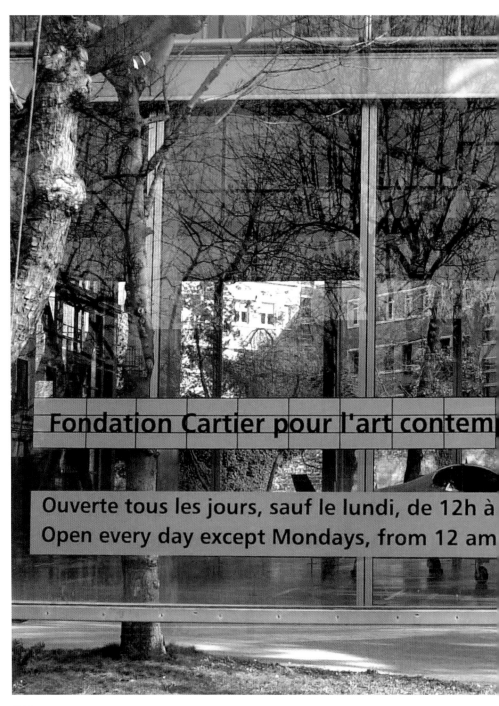

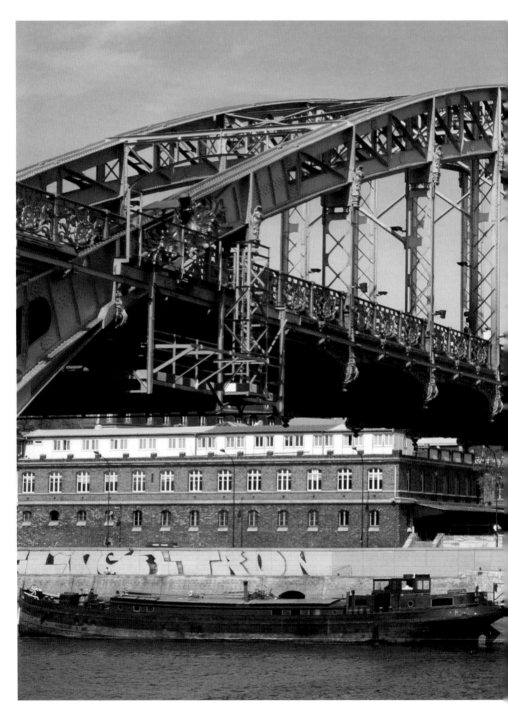

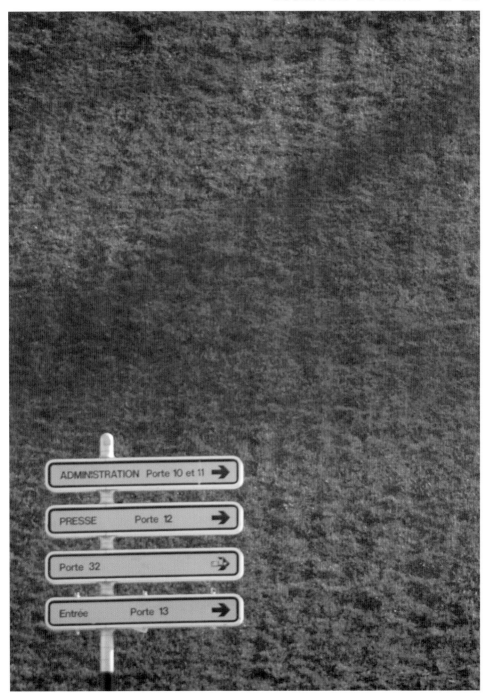

786

"At seven-thirty this morning a bum on the metro wakes up and asks me the time, and since I might assume from his look that he is going to be late, he protests, 'Oh, no, not me, I'm as free as a bird!' Even though we are reading newspapers with opposing views, a worker in blue overalls, smiles at me and says, 'Not us.'"

Marcel Jouhandeau

66This town, which I call secret because foreigners can't penetrate it and which I am tempted to call sacred because its sufferings have made it even dearer to us; this town which Parisians know so well and find its existence so normal that they don't even think to talk about it, except for novelists and poets whose role it is to see, as if for the first time, with fresh eyes, what we take for granted.99

Julien Green

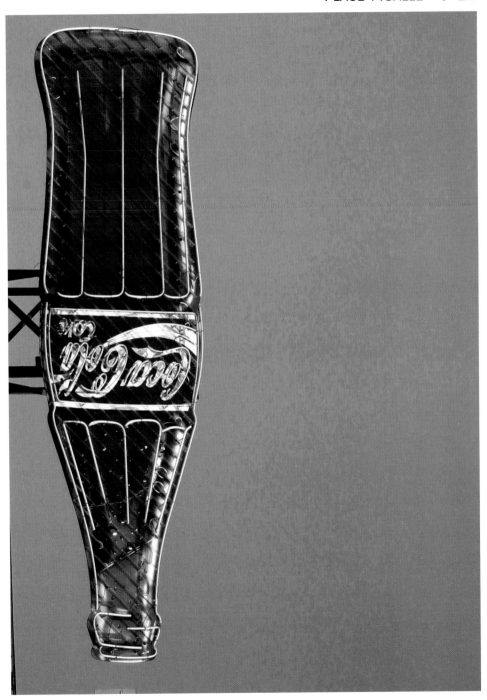

" We live a little bit cloistered in this particular corner of the 10th arrondissement. Wedged between two train stations, inured to the incessant traffic, we often see foreigners who, stepping off the train, think they are going towards Odéon when they are actually going in the opposite direction, toward la Vilette. This makes us shy away from travel. One could say that with so much arriving we fear departures. **"**

Éric Holder

66 It is said of Paris that it is a city on the move, endlessly renewing itself. But the invincible force that allows the names of streets, plazas or theatres to remain despite all the topographical shifts, is here no less important than the durability of the structure of the city. How many times have they torn down one of those little theatres that used to line the Boulevard du Temple, only to see it resurrect in another part of town? (I am loath to use the word sector.) How many streets still preserve the names of landowners who, centuries ago, owned the land where those streets were carved? The name Château d'Eau, an ancient fountain that disappeared long ago, still haunts many a neighborhood today. 99

Walter Benjamin

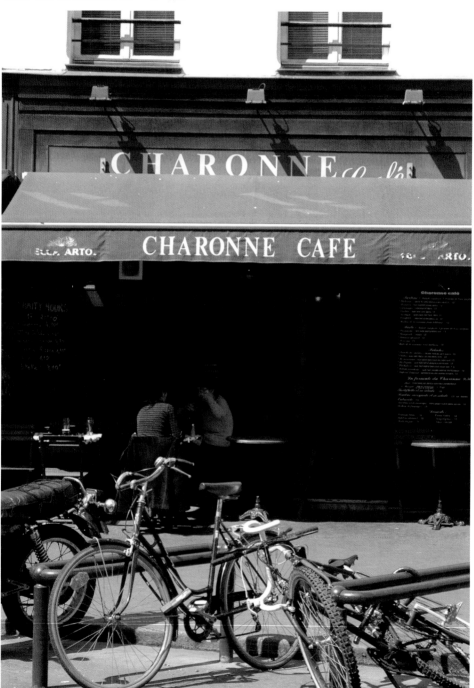

66 Paris has become a monster spread out over an entire region, a biological monster of the most elemental type, a protoplasm, a giant puddle. **99**

Le Corbusier

845

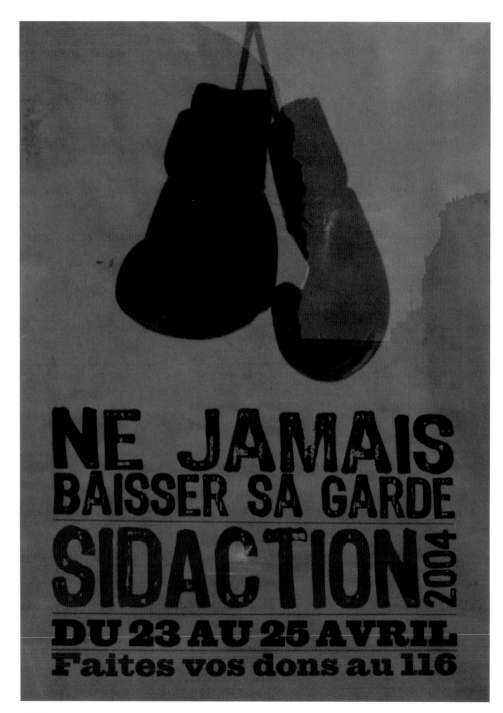

854

66 Everyone has his own picture of this adored City of Light, whether he be a foreigner, a Frenchman, or a born and bred Parisian. For me, a child of the suburb of Ménilmontant which, when I was born there in 1888, was a part of the belt of high hills around the great city, Paris meant only my own neighborhood of working men and artisans and their families. Many of us who were born there had never gone down into the heart of town, just as some country people never know any village but their own. 99

Maurice Chevalier

EWAS ANDRÉAS DUPONT IN THE FILM *MOULIN ROUGE* (1930)

❝Oh! You want to know whether I was born in Paris?... No, at Saint Flour. I said that I was Parisian because, for me, to be 'Parisian' doesn't mean to be born here, but to be reborn here. To be from Paris doesn't necessarily mean having first seen the light of day here, but to see clearly here. There are many foreigners who are very Parisian, and many Parisians who are a bit provincial.**❞**

Sacha Guitry

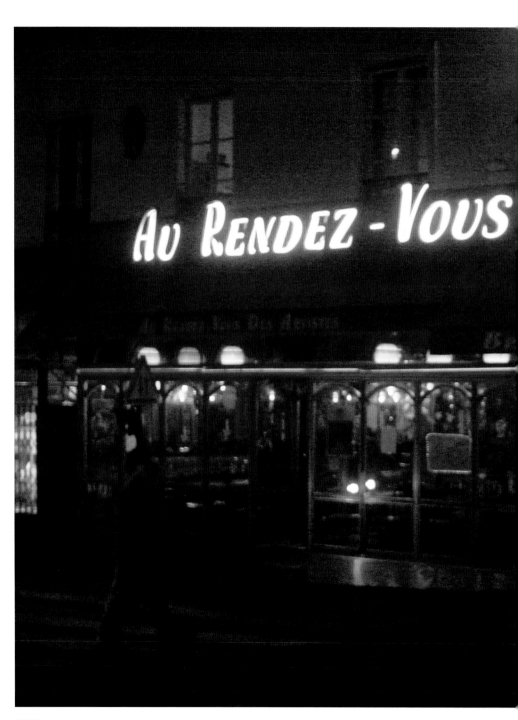

" As long as we are in Montmartre, we might as well stay here... And see the Place du Tertre—that little village square that could only be in Montmartre, which itself can be nowhere but in Paris —and what is more, is indispensable to it. "

Sacha Guitry

COR JESU SAC

"The developers have come calling in the best parts of town. I prefer neighborhoods where the houses have different anatomies. I only feel well in streets where one is likely to see a retiree with a white dog, a florist, a boy on skates, and a fat man, at the same time."

Robert Doisneau

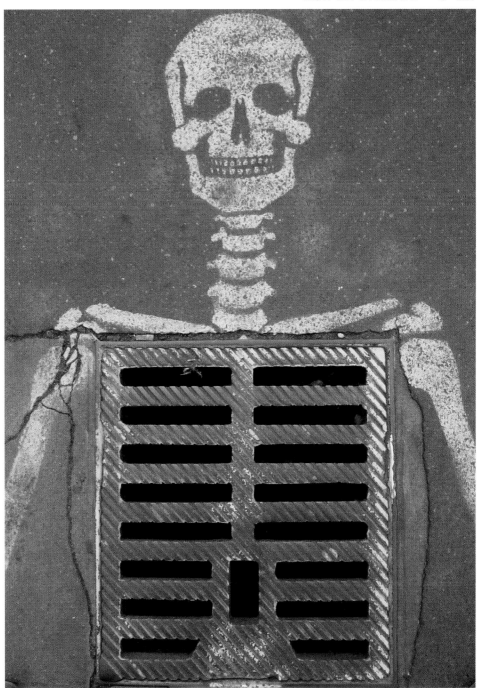

THE PALAIS-ROYAL-MUSÉE DU LOUVRE METRO STATION- 1ˢᵗ arr.

66For the ordinary Parisian, the crucial moment of revelation comes when having understood how one transfers form one line to another, he realizes that his ticket opens up an immense labyrinth, and with it the whole city.99

Michel Tournier

66 People are always amazed if you don't leave Paris during the summer, without understanding that it is precisely because they are gone that you stay. 99

Henry de Montherlant

918

Appendixes

Hotels

Apartment Living in Paris ★★★
47, Avenue de Ségur
75007 Paris
Tel.: (+33) 1 45 67 27 90
Fax: (+33) 1 40 66 60 90
E-mail : apartment.living@
wanadoo.fr
www.apartment-living.com

Atelier Montparnasse ★★★
49, Rue Vavin
75006 Paris
Tel.: (+33) 1 46 33 60 00
Fax: (+33) 1 40 51 04 21
E-mail : hotel@ateliermontparnasse.
com
www.l-ateliermontparnasse.com

Beaumarchais ★★★
3, Rue Oberkampf
75011 Paris
Tel.: (+33) 1 53 36 86 86
Fax: (+33) 1 43 38 32 86
E-mail : reservation@
hotelbeaumarchais.com
www.hotelbeaumarchais.com

Bel-Ami ★★★★
7-11, Rue Saint-Benoît
75006 Paris
Tel.: (+33) 1 42 61 53 53
Fax: (+33) 1 49 27 09 33
E-mail : contact@hotel-bel-ami.com
www.hotel-bel-ami.com

Concorde Saint-Lazare ★★★★
108, Rue Saint-Lazare
75008 Paris
Tel.: (+33) 1 40 08 44 44
Fax: (+33) 1 42 93 (+33) 1 20
E-mail : stlazare@
concordestlazare-paris.com
www.concordestlazare-paris.com

Four Seasons Hôtel ★★★★ LUXE
George V
31, Avenue George-V
75008 Paris
Tel.: (+33) 1 49 52 70 00
Fax: (+33) 1 49 52 70 10

E-mail : resparis@fourseasons.com
www.fourseasons.com

Hôtel Costes ★★★★
239, Rue Saint-Honoré
75001 Paris
Tel.: (+33) 1 42 44 50 00
Fax: (+33) 1 45 44 50 01
www.hotelcostes.com

Hôtel d'Angleterre ★★★
44, Rue Jacob
75006 Paris
Tel.: (+33) 1 42 60 34 72
Fax: (+33) 1 42 60 16 93
E-mail : reservation@hotel-
dangleterre.com
www.hotel-dangleterre.com

Hôtel de Crillon ★★★★
10, Place de la Concorde
75008 Paris
Tel.: (+33) 1 44 71 15 00
Fax: (+33) 1 44 71 15 02
E-mail : crillon@crillon.com
www.crillon-paris.com

Hôtel des Canettes ★★
17, Rue des Canettes
75006 Paris
Tel.: (+33) 1 46 33 12 67
Fax: (+33) 1 46 34 05 06
E-mail : hoteldescanettes@
wanadoo.fr
www.parishotelcanettes.com

Hôtel des Marronniers ★★★
21, Rue Jacob
75006 Paris
Tel.: (+33) 1 43 25 30 60
Fax: (+33) 1 40 46 83 56
E-mail : hotel-des-marronniers@
wanadoo.fr
www.paris-hotel-marronniers.com

Hôtel Jeanne d'Arc ★★
3, Rue de Jarente
75004 Paris
Tel.: (+33) 1 48 87 62 11
Fax: (+33) 1 48 87 37 31

E-mail : information@
hoteljeannedarc.com
www.hoteljeannedarc.com

Hôtel Lancaster ✶✶✶✶
7, Rue de Berri
75008 Paris
Tel.: (+33) 1 40 76 40 76
Fax: (+33) 1 40 76 40 00
E-mail : reservations@hotel-
lancaster.fr
www.hotel-lancaster.fr

Hôtel La Tour Notre-Dame ✶✶✶
20, Rue du Sommerard
75005 Paris
Tel.: (+33) 1 43 54 47 60
Fax: (+33) 1 43 26 42 34
E-mail : tour-notre-dame@magic.fr
www.hotels-la-tour.com

Hôtel Meurice ✶✶✶✶
228, Rue de Rivoli
75001 Paris
Tel.: (+33) 1 44 58 10 10
Fax: (+33) 1 44 52 10 17
E-mail : reservations@meuricehotel.com
www.meuricehotel.com

Hôtel Montalembert ✶✶✶✶
3, Rue de Montalembert
75007 Paris
Tel.: (+33) 1 45 49 68 68
Fax: (+33) 1 45 49 69 49
E-mail : welcome@montalembert.
com
www.montalembert.com

Hôtel Raphael ✶✶✶✶
17, Avenue Kléber
75016 Paris
Tel.: (+33) 1 44 28 00 28
Fax: (+33) 1 45 (+33) 1 21 50
E-mail : management@raphael-
hotel.com
www.raphael-hotel.com

La Trémoille ✶✶✶✶
14, Rue de la Trémoille
75008 Paris

Tel.: (+33) 1 56 52 14 00
Fax: (+33) 1 40 70 01 08
E-mail : reservation@hotel-
tremoille.com
www.hotel-tremoille.com

Le Bristol ✶✶✶✶
112, Rue du Faubourg-Saint-
Honoré
75008 Paris
Tel.: (+33) 1 53 43 43 00
Fax: (+33) 1 53 43 43 01
E-mail : resa@hotel-bristol.com
www.hotel-bristol.com

Le Lavoisier ✶✶✶✶
21, Rue Lavoisier
75008 Paris
Tel.: (+33) 1 53 30 06 06
Fax: (+33) 1 53 30 23 00
www.parischarmhotels.com

L'Hôtel ✶✶✶✶
13, Rue des Beaux-Arts
75006 Paris
Tel.: (+33) 1 44 41 99 00
Fax: (+33) 1 43 25 64 81
E-mail : reservation@l-hotel.com
www.l-hotel.com

Lutetia ✶✶✶✶
45, Boulevard Raspail
75007 Paris
Tel.: (+33) 1 49 54 46 46
Fax: (+33) 1 49 54 46 00
E-mail : lutetia-paris@lutetia-
paris.com
www.lutetia-paris.com

Normandy ✶✶✶✶
7, Rue de l'Échelle
75001 Paris
Tel.: (+33) 1 42 60 30 21
Fax: (+33) 1 42 60 17 09
E-mail : normandy@hotelsparis.fr
www.hotelsparis.fr

Park Hyatt ✶✶✶✶
5, Rue de la Paix
75002 Paris

Tel.: (+33) 1 58 71 12 34
Fax: (+33) 1 58 71 12 35
E-mail : vendome@paris.hyatt.com
www.paris.vendome.hyatt.com

Pavillon de la Reine ★★★★
28, Place des Vosges
75003 Paris
Tel.: (+33) 1 40 29 19 19
Fax: (+33) 1 40 29 19 20
E-mail : contact@pavillon-de-la-
reine.com
www.pavillon-de-la-reine.com

Pershing Hall ★★★★
49, Rue Pierre-Charron
75008 Paris
Tel.: (+33) 1 58 36 58 00
Fax: (+33) 1 58 36 58 01
E-mail : info@pershinghall.com
www.pershinghall.com

Plaza-Athénée ★★★★ LUXE
25, Avenue Montaigne
75008 Paris
Tel.: (+33) 1 53 67 66 65
Fax: (+33) 1 53 67 66 65
E-mail : reservation@plaza-
athenee-paris.com
www.plaza-athenee-paris.com

Regina ★★★★
2, Place des Pyramides
75001 Paris
Tel.: (+33) 1 42 60 31 10
Fax: (+33) 1 40 15 95 16
E-mail : reservations@regina-
hotel.com
www.regina-hotel.com

Ritz Paris ★★★★ LUXE
15, Place Vendôme
75001 Paris
Tel.: (+33) 1 43 16 30 30
Fax: (+33) 1 43 16 31 78
E-mail : resa@ritzparis.com
www.ritz.com

Saint-James Paris ★★★★
43, Avenue Bugeaud

75016 Paris
Tel.: (+33) 1 44 05 81 81
Fax: (+33) 1 53 65 66 88
E-mail : contact@saint-james-
paris.com
www.saint-james-paris.com

Square ★★★★
3, Rue de Boulainvilliers
75016 Paris
Tel.: (+33) 1 44 14 91 90
Fax: (+33) 1 44 14 91 99
E-mail : reservation@
hotelsquare.com
www.hotelsquare.com

Trocadéro Dokhan's ★★★★
117, Rue Lauriston
75016 Paris
Tel.: (+33) 1 53 65 66 99
Fax. : (+33) 1 56 65 66 88
E-mail : hotel.trocadero.dokhans
@wanadoo.fr

Villa Royale ★★★★
2, Rue Duperré
75009 Paris
Tel.: (+33) 1 55 31 78 78
Fax: (+33) 1 55 31 78 70
E-mail : royale@leshotelsdeparis.
com
www.leshotelsdeparis.com

Villa Saint-Germain ★★★★
29, Rue Jacob
75006 Paris
Tel.: (+33) 1 43 26 60 00
Fax: (+33) 1 46 34 63 63
E-mail : hotel@villa-
saintgermain.com
www.villa-saintgermain.com

Westminster ★★★★
13, Rue de la Paix
75002 Paris
Tel.: (+33) 1 42 61 57 46
Fax: (+33) 1 42 60 0 66
E-mail : resa.westminster@
warwickhotels.com
www.hotelwestminster.com

Restaurants
Cafes

6 New York
6 Avenue de New York
75016 Paris
Tel: (+33) 1 40 70 03 30

Alain Ducasse au Plaza Athénée
25 Avenue Montaigne
75008 Paris
Tel: (+33) 1 53 67 65 00

Anahi
49 Rue Volta
75003 Paris
Tel: (+33) 1 48 87 88 24

Angelina
226 Rue de Rivoli
75001 Paris
Tel: (+33) 1 42 60 82 00

Au Bon Accueil
14 Rue Monttessuy
75007 Paris
Tel: (+33) 1 47 05 46 11

Aux Lyonnais
32 Rue Saint-Marc
75002 Paris
Tel: (+33) 1 42 96 65 04

Bofinger
5 Rue de la Bastille
75004 Paris
Tel: (+33) 1 42 72 87 82

Brasserie Lipp
151 Boulevard Saint-Germain
75006 Paris
Tel: (+33) 1 45 48 53 91

Caffé Armani
149 Boulevard Saint-Germain
75006 Paris
Tel: (+33) 1 45 48 62 15

Café Beaubourg
43 Rue Saint-Merri
75004 Paris
Tel: (+33) 1 48 87 63 96

Café Blanc
40 Rue François 1er
75008 Paris
Tel: (+33) 1 53 67 30 13

Café de Flore
172 Boulevard Saint-Germain
75006 Paris
Tel: (+33) 1 45 48 55 26

Café de l'Esplanade
52 Rue Faubert
75007 Paris
Tel: (+33) 1 47 05 38 50

Café Étienne Marcel
34 Rue Étienne Marcel
75002 Paris
Tel: (+33) 1 45 08 01 03

Café Les Deux Magots
6 Place Saint-Germain-des-Près
75006 Paris
Tel: (+33) 1 45 48 55 25

Café Marly
93 Rue de Rivoli
Cour Napoléon
Louvre
75001 Paris
Tel: (+33) 1 49 26 06 60

Café Maure
Mosque of Paris
39 Rue Geoffroy-Saint-Hilaire
75005 Paris
Tel: (+33) 1 43 31 18 14

Castel
15 Rue Princesse
75006 Paris
Tel: (+33) 1 40 51 52 80

Caviar Kaspia
17 Place de la Madeleine
75008 Paris
Tel: (+33) 1 42 65 33 32

Chez Georges
1 Rue du Mail
75002 Paris
Tel: (+33) 1 42 60 07 11

Chez Prune
71 Quai de Valmy
75010 Paris
Tel: (+33) 1 42 41 30 47

Cristal Room
Maison Baccarat
11 Place des États-Unis
75016 Paris
Tel: (+33) 1 40 22 11 10

Davé
12 Rue de Richelieu
75001 Paris
Tel: (+33) 1 42 60 96 18

Georges
Georges-Pompidou Center, 6th Floor
Place Beaubourg
75004 Paris
Tel: (+33) 1 44 78 47 99

Guy Savoy
18 Rue Troyan
75017 Paris
Tel: (+33) 1 43 80 40 61

Hôtel Costes
239 Rue Saint-Honoré
75001 Paris
Tel: (+33) 1 42 44 50 00

Issé
56 Rue Sainte-Anne
75002 Paris
Tel: (+33) 1 42 96 67 76

Joe's
Joseph
277 Rue Saint-Honoré
75008 Paris
Tel: (+33) 1 49 27 05 54

Joe Allen
30 Rue Pierre-Lescot
75001 Paris
Tel: (+33) 1 42 36 70 13

Kinugawa
4 Rue Saint-Philippe-du-Roule
75008 Paris
Tel: (+33) 1 45 63 08 07

Kong
1 Rue Pont Neuf
75001 Paris
Tel: (+33) 1 40 39 09 00

La Coupole
102 Boulevard du Montparnasse
75014 Paris
Tel: (+33) 1 43 20 14 20

Ladurée
16 Rue Royale
75008 Paris
Tel: (+33) 1 42 60 21 79

Ladurée Bonaparte
21 Rue Bonaparte
75006 Paris
Tel: (+33) 1 44 07 64 87

La Maison Blanche
15 Avenue Montaigne
75008 Paris
Tel: (+33) 1 47 23 55 99

L'Ambroisie
9 Place des Vosges
75004 Paris
Tel: (+33) 1 42 78 51 45

L'Ami Louis
32 Rue du Vert-Bois
75003 Paris
Tel: (+33) 1 48 87 77 48

La Maison du Caviar
21 Rue Quentin Bauchart
75008 Paris
Tel: (+33) 1 47 23 53 43

La Palette
43 Rue de Seine
75006 Paris
Tel: (+33) 1 43 26 68 15

L'Arpège
84 Rue de Varenne
75007 Paris
Tel: (+33) 1 45 51 47 33

Lasserre
17 Avenue Franklin Roosevelt
75008 Paris
Tel: (+33) 1 43 59 53 43

L'Assiette
181 Rue Château
75014 Paris
Tel: (+33) 1 43 22 64 86

L'Astrance
4 Rue Beethoven
75016 Paris
Tel: (+33) 1 40 50 84 40

L'Atelier de Joël Robuchon
5 Rue Montalembert
75007 Paris
Tel: (+33) 1 42 22 56 56

La Table de Joël Robuchon
16 Avenue Bugeaud
75016 Paris
Tel: (+33) 1 56 28 16 16

La Tour d'Argent
15-17 Quai de la Tournelle
75005 Paris
Tel: (+33) 1 43 54 23 31

L'Avenue
41 Avenue Montaigne
75008 Paris
Tel: (+33) 1 40 70 14 91

Le 404
69 Rue des Gravilliers
75003 Paris
Tel: (+33) 1 42 74 57 81

Le Bourdonnec Pascal
75 Rue de Seine
75006 Paris
Tel: (+33) 1 43 26 55 15

Le Cherche-Midi
22 Rue du Cherche-Midi
75006 Paris
Tel: (+33) 1 45 48 27 44

Le Cinq
Four Seasons George V
31 Avenue George V
75008 Paris
Tel: (+33) 1 49 52 70 00

Le Comptoir de Thiou
12 Avenue George-V
75008 Paris
Tel: (+33) 1 47 20 89 56

Le Flandrin
80 Avenue Henri-Martin
75016 Paris
Tel: (+33) 1 45 04 34 69

Le Grand Véfour
17 Rue de Beaujolais
75001 Paris
Tel: (+33) 1 42 96 56 27

Le Jules Verne
Restaurant de la Tour Eiffel
Champs de Mars
75007 Paris
Tel: (+33) 1 45 55 61 44

Le Limelight
128 Avenue de France
75013 Paris
Tel: (+33) 1 56 61 44 04

Le Petit Marché
9 Rue de Béarn
75003 Paris
Tel: (+33) 1 42 72 06 67

Le Pichet
68 Rue Pierre Charron
75008 Paris
Tel: (+33) 1 43 59 50 34

Le Pré Catelan
Route de Suresnes
Bois de Boulogne
75016 Paris
Tel: (+33) 1 44 14 41 14

Le Publicis Drugstore
133 Avenue des Champs-Élysées
75008 Paris
Tel: (+33) 1 44 43 79 00

Le Raphael
Hôtel Raphael
17 Avenue Kleber
75016 Paris
Tel: (+33) 1 53 64 32 00

Le Relais
Plaza Athénée
25 Avenue Montaigne
75008 Paris
Tel: (+33) 1 53 67 66 65

Le Stella
133 Avenue Victor Hugo
75016 Paris
Tel: (+33) 1 56 90 56 00

Le Stresa
7 Rue des Gravilliers
75003 Paris
Tel: (+33) 1 47 23 51 62

Le Voltaire
27 Quai Voltaire
75007 Paris
Tel: (+33) 1 42 61 17 49

Le Waterbar
Colette
213 Rue Saint-Honoré
75001 Paris
Tel: (+33) 1 55 35 33 93

Le Zéphyr
1 Rue du Jourdain
75020 Parirs
Tel: (+33) 1 46 36 65 81

L'Ostéria
10 Rue de Sévigné
75004 Paris
Tel: (+33) 1 42 71 37 08

Lucas Carton
9 Place de la Madeleine
75008 Paris
Tel: (+33) 1 42 65 22 90

Maison Prunier
16 Avenue Victor Hugo
75116 Paris
Tel: (+33) 1 44 17 35 85

Market
15 Avenue Matignon
75008 Paris
Tel: (+33) 1 56 43 40 90

Michel Rostang
20 Rue Rennequin
75017 Paris
Tel: (+33) 1 47 63 40 77

Montalembert
Hôtel Revu
3 Rue de Montalembert
75007 Paris
Tel: (+33) 1 45 49 68 68

Pierre Gagnaire
Hôtel Balzac
6 Rue Balzac
75008 Paris
Tel: (+33) 1 44 35 18 25

Restaurant Chartier
7 Rue Faubourg Montmartre
75009 Paris
Tel: (+33) 1 47 70 86 29

Sormani
4 Rue du Général-Lanrezac
75017 Paris
Tel: (+33) 1 43 80 13 91

Spoon Food
14 Rue de Marignan
75008 Paris
Tel: (+33) 1 40 76 36 66

Ze Kitchen Gallery
4 Rue des Grands-Augustins
75006 Paris
Tel: (+33) 1 44 32 00 32

Bars
Clubs

Balajo
9 Rue de Lappe
75011 Paris
Tel: (+33) 1 47 00 07 87

Bar Hemingway
Ritz Paris
15 Place Vendôme
75001 Paris
Tel: (+33) 1 43 16 33 65

Bataclan
50 Boulevard Voltaire
75011 Paris
Tel: (+33) 1 43 14 35 35

Cabaret/Le Cab
2 Place Palais-Royal
75001 Paris
Tel: (+33) 1 58 62 56 25

Castel
15 Rue Princesse
75006 Paris
Tel: (+33) 1 40 51 52 80

Élysée-Montmartre
72 Boulevard de Rochechouart
75018 Paris
Tel: (+33) 892 692 392

Harry's New York Bar
5 Rue Daunou
75002 Paris
Tel: (+33) 1 42 61 71 14

La Cigale
120 Boulevard Rochechouart
75018 Paris
Tel: (+33) 1 49 25 81 75

Le Bar du Plaza Athénée
25 Avenue Montaigne
75008 Paris
Tel: (+33) 1 53 67 66 65

Le Bar des Théâtres
6 Avenue Montaigne
75008 Paris
Tel: (+33) 1 47 23 34 63

Les Bains
7 Rue du Bourg-l'Abbé
75003 Paris
Tel: (+33) 1 48 87 07 80

Le Divan du Monde
75 Rue des Martyrs
75018 Paris
Tel: (+33) 1 42 52 02 46

L'Étoile
12 Rue de Presbourg
75016 Paris
Tel: (+33) 1 45 00 78 70

Man Ray
32 Rue Marbeuf
75008 Paris
Tel: (+33) 1 56 88 36 36

Maxim's
3 Rue Royale
75008 Paris
Tel: (+33) 1 42 65 27 94

Queen
102 Avenue des Champs-Élysées
75008 Paris
Tel: (+33) 1 53 89 08 90

Régine's
49-51 Rue de Ponthieu
75008 Paris
Tel: (+33) 1 43 59 21 13

VIP Room
76 Avenue Champs-Élysées
75008 Paris
Tel: (+33) 1 56 69 16 66

Markets
Flea Markets
Department stores

Galeries Lafayette
40 Boulevard Haussmann
75009 Paris
Tel: (+33) 1 42 82 34 56

Grande Épicerie
38 Rue de Sèvres
75006 Paris
Tel: (+33) 1 44 38 81 01

La Samaritaine
19 Rue Monnaie
75001 Paris
Tel: (+33) 1 40 41 20 20

Le Bon Marché
24 Rue de Sèvres
75007 Paris
Tel: (+33) 1 44 39 80 00

Le Printemps
64 Boulevard Haussmann
75009 Paris
Tel: (+33) 1 42 82 50 00

Bird Market
Place Louis-Lépine
75004 Paris
Open Sunday from 9am to 7pm.

Flower Market
Place Louis-Lépine,
on the Île de la Cité
75004 Paris
Open every day except Sunday,
from 8am to 7pm.

Used and Old Book Market
Rue des Morillons
in the Parc Georges-Brassens
75015 Paris
Open every weekend
from 9am to 6pm.

Marché Hédiard
21 Place de la Madeleine
75008 Paris
Tel: (+33) 1 43 12 88 88

Marché Saint-Pierre
2 Rue Charles-Nodier
75018 Paris
Tel: (+33) 1 46 06 92 25
Open Monday from 1:30pm to
6:30pm, and Tuesday through
Saturday from 10am to 6:30pm.

Clignancourt Flea Market
Rue des Rosiers
75018 Paris
Metro Porte de Clignancourt
Open Saturday, Sunday and
Monday, all day.

Montreuil Flea Market
Avenue de la Porte de Montreuil
75020 Paris
Metro Porte de Montreuil
Open Saturday, Sunday and
Monday from 7am to 7:30pm.

Antique Dealers

Didier Aaron & Cie
118, Rue du Faubourg-Saint-Honoré
75008 Paris
Tél. : 01 47 42 47 34

Alb Antiquités
3, Rue de Lille
75007 Paris
Tél. : 01 47 03 45 58

Éric Allart
5, Rue de Beaune
75007 Paris
Tél. : 01 42 61 31 44

L'Arc-en-Seine
27 and 31, Rue de Seine
75006 Paris
Tél. : 01 43 29 11 02

Aveline
94, Rue du Faubourg-Saint-Honoré
Place Beauvau
75008 Paris
Tél. : 01 42 66 60 29

Eugène Becker
136, Rue du Faubourg-Saint-Honoré
75008 Paris
Tél. : 01 42 89 44 9

Alexandre Biaggi
14, Rue de Seine
75006 Paris
Tél. : 01 44 07 34 730

Galerie Chastel-Maréchal
5, Rue Bonaparte
75006 Paris
Tél. : 01 40 46 82 61

Jean-Louis Danant
36, Avenue Matignon
75008 Paris
Tél. : 01 42 89 40 15

Galerie Danbon-Pokorny
25, Rue de Lille
75007 Paris
Tél. : 01 40 20 01 79

Ariane Dandois
92, Rue du Faubourg-Saint-Honoré
75008 Paris
Tél. : 01 43 12 39 39

Luc Debruille
3, Rue de Lille
75007 Paris
Tél. : 01 42 61 78 72

Stéphane Deschamps
19, Rue Guénégaud
75006 Paris
Tél. : 0146 33 58 00

Denis Doria
16, Rue de Seine
75006 Paris
Tél. : 01 43 54 73 49

Galerie Down Town
33, Rue de Seine
75006 Paris
Tél. : 01 46 33 82 41

Jean-François Dubois
15, Rue de Lille
75007 Paris
Tél. : 01 42 60 40 17

Galerie Jean-Jacques Dutko
13, Rue Bonaparte
75006 Paris
Tél. : 01 43 26 96 13

Anne-Sophie Duval
5, Quai Malaquais
75006 Paris
Tél. : 01 43 54 51 16

Fabius Frères
152, Boulevard Haussmann
75008 Paris
Tél. : 01 45 62 39 18

Fabre & Fils
19, Rue Balzac
75008 Paris
Tél. : 01 45 61 17 52

Galerie Patrick Fourtin
9, Rue des Bons-Enfants
75001 Paris
Tél. : 01 42 60 12 63

Galerie Yves Gastou
12, Rue Bonaparte
75006 Paris
Tél. : 01 53 73 00 10

Gismondi
20, Rue Royale
75008 Paris
Tél. : 01 42 60 73 89

Marcel Grunspan
6-8, Rue Royale
75008 Paris
Tél. : 01 42 60 57 57

Galerie Jousse-Seguin
34, Rue de Charonne
75011 Paris
Tél. : 01 47 00 32 35

Kraemer & Cie
43, Rue de Monceau
75008 Paris
Tél. : 01 45 63 31 23

J. Kugel
279, Rue Saint-Honoré
75008 Paris
Tél. : 01 42 60 86 23

Galerie Jacques Lacoste
22, Rue de Lille
75007 Paris
Tél. : 01 40 20 81 82

Anne Lajoix
16, Rue des Saints-Pères
75007 Paris
Tél. : 01 42 86 90 94

François Léage
178, Rue du Faubourg-Saint-Honoré
75008 Paris
Tél. : 01 45 63 43 46

Étienne Lévy
178, Rue du Faubourg-Saint-Honoré
75008 Paris
Tél. : 01 45 44 65 50

Jean Lupu
43, Rue du Faubourg-Saint-Honoré
75008 Paris
Tél. : 01 42 65 93 19

Félix Marcilhac
8, Rue Bonaparte
75006 Paris
Tél. : 01 43 26 47 36

Michel Meyer
24, Avenue Matignon
75008 Paris
Tél. : 01 42 66 62 95

Yves Mikaeloff
10, Rue Royale
75008 Paris
Tél. : 01 42 61 64 42

Joëlle Mortier-Valat
13, Rue des Saints-Pères
75007 Paris
Tél. : 01 42 60 28 30

Jean-Pierre Orinel
12, Rue de Lille
75007 Paris
Tél. : 01 42 97 58 66

Galerie du Passage
20-22, Galerie Véro-Dodat
75001 Paris
Tél. : 01 42 36 01 13

Galerie Perrin
98, Rue du Faubourg-Saint-Honoré
75008 Paris
Tél. : 01 42 65 01 38

Philippe Perrin
3, Quai Voltaire
75007 Paris
Tél. : 01 42 60 27 20

Galerie Éric Philippe
25, Galerie Véro-Dodat
75001 Paris
Tél. : 01 42 33 28 26

Galerie Plaisance
3, Rue Bonaparte
75006 Paris
Tél. : 01 43 29 05 38

Maroun H. Salloum
17 bis, Quai Voltaire
75007 Paris
Tél. : 01 40 15 95 01

Segoura
14, Place François-Ier
75008 Paris
Tél. : 01 42 89 20 20

Patrick Serraire
30, Rue de Lille
75007 Paris
Tél. : 01 47 03 43 13

Bernard Steinitz
9, Rue du Cirque
75008 Paris
Tél. : 01 42 89 40 50

Vallois
41, Rue de Seine
75006 Paris
Tél. : 01 43 29 50 84

Jacques de Vos
7, Rue Bonaparte
75006 Paris
Tél. : 01 43 29 88 94

Galerie Olivier Watelet
11, Rue Bonaparte
75006 Paris
Tél. : 01 43 26 07 87

Museums
Galleries
Auction Houses

Artcurial
7 Rond-Point des Champs-Élysées
75008 Paris
Tel: (+33) 1 42 99 16 19

Centre Georges Pompidou
Christie's
9 Avenue Matignon
75008 Paris
Tel: (+33) 1 40 76 85 85

Drouot
9 Rue Drouot
75009 Paris
Tél. : 01 44 78 12 33

Christie's
9, Avenue Matignon
75008 Paris
Tél. : 01 40 76 85 85

Cité des Sciences et de l'Industrie
30, Avenue Corentin-Cariou
75019 Paris
Tél. : 01 40 05 70 00

Drouot
9, Rue Drouot
75009 Paris
Tél. : 01 48 00 20 20

Étude Tajan
37, Rue des Mathurins
75008 Paris
Tél. : 01 53 30 30 30

Fondation Cartier
261, boulevard Raspail
75014 Paris
Tél. : 01 42 18 56 50

Fondation Dina Vierny
59, Rue de Grenelle
75007 Paris
Tél. : 01 42 22 59 58

Galerie Nationale
du Jeu de Paume
Place de la Concorde
75008 Paris
Tél. : 01 47 03 12 50

Grand-Palais
21, Avenue Franklin-D.-Roosevelt
75008 Paris
Tél. : 01 43 59 76 78
Institut du Monde Arabe
1, Rue des Fossés-Saint-Bernard
75005 Paris
Tél. : 01 40 1 38 38

Maison Européenne
de la Photographie
5-7, Rue de Fourcy
75004 Paris
Tél. : 01 44 78 75 00

Mona Bismarck Foundation
34, Avenue de New York
75116 Paris
Tél. : 01 47 23 38 88

Musée Albert-Kahn
14 Rue du Port
92100 Boulogne
Tél. : 01 46 04 52 80

Musée d'Art moderne
de la Ville de Paris
11, Avenue du Président-Wilson
75016 Paris
Tél. : 01 53 67 40 00

Musée de l'Érotisme
72, boulevard de Clichy
75018 Paris
Tél. : 01 42 58 28 73

Musée de la Musique
Porte de Pantin
221, Avenue Jean-Jaurès
75019 Paris
Tél. : 01 44 84 45 00

Musée de la Vie romantique
16, Rue Chaptal
75009 Paris
Tél. : 01 55 31 95 67

Musée des Arts décoratifs
107, Rue de Rivoli
75001 Paris
Tél. : 01 44 55 57 50

Musée des Arts et Métiers
60, Rue Réaumur
75003 Paris
Tél. : 01 53 01 82 00

Louvre Museum
34, Quai du Louvre
75001 Paris
Tél. : 01 40 20 50 50

Musée du Quai Branly
Ouverture en 2005
Bureaux provisoires :
15, Rue Jean-Baptiste Berlier
75013 Paris
Tél. : 01 56 61 70 00

Musée en Herbe
Jardin d'Acclimatation
Bois de Boulogne
75116 Paris
Tél. : 01 40 67 97 66

Musée Eugène Delacroix
6, Rue de Furstenberg
75006 Paris
Tél. : 01 44 41 86 50

Musée Galliera
10, Avenue Pierre-Ier-de-Serbie
75016 Paris
Tél. : 01 56 52 86 00

Musée Grévin
10, Boulevard Montmartre
75009 Paris
Tél. : 01 47 70 85 05

Musée Guimet
6, Place d'Iéna
75016 Paris
Tél. : 01 56 52 53 00

Musée Gustave Moreau
14, Rue de La Rochefoucauld
75009 Paris
Tél. : 01 48 74 38 50

Musée Jacquemart-André
158, Boulevard Haussmann
75008 Paris
Tél. : 01 42 89 04 91

Musée Maillol
61, Rue de Grenelle
75007 Paris
Tél. : 01 42 22 59 58

Musée Marmottan-Monet
2, Rue Louis-Boilly
75016 Paris
Tél. : 01 44 96 50 33

Musée national de la Marine
Place du Trocadéro
75116 Paris
Tél. : 01 53 65 69 69

Musée national du Moyen-Âge
6, place Paul-Painlevé
75005 Paris
Tél. : 01 53 73 78 00

Musée Nissim de Camondo
63, Rue de Monceau
75017 Paris
Tél. : 01 53 89 06 40

**Museum National
d'Histoire Naturelle**
57, Rue Cuvier
75005 Paris
Tél. : 01 40 79 30 00

Orsay Museum
1, Rue de la Légion-d'Honneur
75007 Paris
Tél. : 01 40 49 48 14

Palais de la Découverte
Avenue Franklin-D.-Roosevelt
75008 Paris
Tél. : 01 56 43 20 21

Palais de la Porte Dorée
293, Avenue Daumesnil
75012 Paris
Tél. : 01 44 74 84 80

Palais de Tokyo
13, Avenue du Président-Wilson
75016 Paris
Tél. : 01 47 23 38 86

Pavillon de l'Arsenal
21, boulevard Morland
75004 Paris
Tél. : 01 42 76 33 97

Petit-Palais
1, Avenue Dutuit
75008 Paris
Tél. : 01 44 51 19 31

Picasso Museum
5, Rue de Thorigny
75003 Paris
Tél. : 01 42 71 25 21

Rodin Museum
77, Rue de Varenne
75007 Paris
Tél. : 01 44 18 61 10

Sotheby's
76, Rue du Faubourg-Saint-Honoré
75008 Paris
Tél. : 01 53 05 53 05

Embassies
Services

BABY-SITTING
Allo Maman Dépannage
38 Rue Greuze
75116 Paris
Tel: (+33) 1 47 55 15 75

BEAUTY
Le Hammam de la Mosquée
C.C.M.P.
39 Rue Geoffroy-Saint-Hilaire
75005 Paris
Tel: (+33) 1 43 31 18 14

COMPUTERS/PHONES
A'loc
Computer leasing
141 Boulevard du Montparnasse
75006 Paris
Tel: (+33) 1 53 10 09 40

Rent a Cell Express
14 Rue Magellan
75008 Paris
Tel: (+33) 1 53 93 78 00

DOCTORS
S.O.S Médecins Paris
87 Boulevard Port-Royal
75013 Paris
Tel: (+33) 1 43 37 77 77

S.O.S Médecins Neuilly
27 Rue de Sèvres
92100 Boulogne Billancourt
Tel: (+33) 1 46 03 77 44

EMBASSIES
The Embassy of Belgium
9 Rue Tilsitt
75017 Paris
Tel: (+33) 1 44 09 39 39

The Embassy of Germany
13 Avenue Franklin D. Roosevelt
75008 Paris
Tel: (+33) 1 53 83 45 00

The Embassy of Great Britain
35 Rue du Faubourg Saint-Honoré
75008 Paris
Tel: (+33) 1 44 51 31 00

The Embassy of Italy
51 Rue Varenne
75007 Paris
Tel: (+33) 1 49 54 03 00

The Embassy of Japan
7 Avenue Hoche
75008 Paris
Tel: (+33) 1 48 88 62 00

The Embassy of Spain
22 Avenue Marceau
75008 Paris
Tel: (+33) 1 44 43 18 00

The Embassy of the United States
2 Rue Saint-Florentin
75001 Paris
Tel: (+33) 1 43 12 22 22

The Embassy of Russia
40 Boulevard Lannes
75116 Paris
Tel: (+33) 1 45 04 05 50

FLOWER SHOPS
Vogel Lagneau 24h/24
2 Rue de Marignan
75008 Paris
Tel: (+33) 1 47 23 42 67

HOSPITALS
American Hospital of Paris
63 Boulevard Victor Hugo
92200 Neuilly sur Seine
Tel: (+33) 1 46 41 25 25

Hôpital Lariboisière
2 Rue Ambroise Paré
75010 Paris
Tel: (+33) 1 49 95 65 65

Hôpital Pitié Salpêtière
47 Boulevard Hôpital
75013 Paris
Tel: (+33) 1 42 16 00 00

LUGGAGE REPAIR
Malles Bertaux
135 Rue d'Aboukir
75002 Paris
Tel: (+33) 1 42 33 03 80

PHARMACIES
Publicis Drugstore
133 Avenue des Champs-Élysées
75008 Paris
Tel: (+33) 1 47 20 39 25

Pharmacie Les Champs 24 h/24
84 Avenue des Champs-Élysées
75008 Paris
Tel: (+33) 1 45 62 02 41

Pharma Presto 24 h/24
Tel: (+33) 1 42 42 42 50

NEWSPAPERS AND MAGAZINES
Publicis Drugstore
133 Avenue des Champs-Élysées
75008 Paris
Tel: (+33) 1 44 43 79 00

PRESSING/SEWING
Nestor Services
6 bis Rue Jonquoy
75014 Paris
Tel: (+33) 801 630 600

TAXIS/CHAUFFEURS/MOTO-TAXIS
Appel Taxis
8 Boulevard Malesherbes
75008 Paris
Tel: (+33) 1 42 65 00 00

Citybird
37 Avenue de Versailles
75016 Paris
Tel: 0826 100 100

Taxi Driver Prestige
239 Rue Faubourg Saint-Honoré
75008 Paris
Tel: (+33) 1 53 81 00 15

Taxis G7
Tel: (+33) 1 47 39 47 39

TICKET SALES
Ticketnet
Tel: (+33) 892 390 100

Marivaux
7 Rue de Marivaux
75002 Paris
Tel: (+33) 1 42 97 46 70

TRAVEL ORGANIZERS
VIP Visas Express
Tel: (+33) 1 44 10 72 72
www.visas-express.com

Parisian Walks

VIEWS

From the terrace of the Palais de Chaillot one can admire the Eiffel Tower across the Seine, the École Militaire, the Trocadéro...

From the Pont Alexandre-III one can contemplate the Invalides, the Grand and the Petit Palais...

Standing by the Obelisk in Place de la Concorde one can see the Champs Elysées, the Arc de Triomphe, the Grande Arche de la Défense, the Church of la Madeleine, the Assemblée Nationale, and the Tuileries Gardens...

PARIS SEEN FROM ABOVE

Eiffel Tower
Tour Montparnasse
Sacré-Cœur
The Platform of the Arc de Triomphe
The Towers of Notre Dame.

THE CANALS

Canal Saint-Martin:

Flowing exclusively through Paris for a length of 3 miles, it crosses the 19th, 10th, 11th, 4th and 12th arrondissements

Canal de l'Ourcq

Originating on the Oise river, at Mareuil-sur-Ourcq, it is 64 miles long and ends in the 19th arrondissement of Paris.

Canal Saint-Denis

It follows its course from the 19th arrondissement of Paris to Saint-Denis in Seine-Saint-Denis, for a total length of 4.4 miles.

BOAT RIDES ON THE CANALS

Canauxrama

13, Quai de la Loire, 19th arr.
(+33) 1 42 39 15 00
www.canauxrama.com

Paris Canal

19, Quai de la Loire, 19th arr.
(+33) 1 42 40 96 97
www.pariscanal.com

THE BRIDGES (FROM EAST TO WEST)

Pont Amont (1969)

12th arrondissement.
Concrete bridge allowing automobiles on the Périphérique to cross the Seine up river from Paris.
Conception: Dambre, Herzog, Long-Depaquit and Rousselin.

Pont National (1853)

12th – 13th arrondissements.
Stone bridge linking the Boulevard Poniatowski to the Boulevard Masséna.
Conception: Couche, Gaspard, Netter and Petit.

Pont de Tolbiac (1882)

12th – 13th arrondissements.
Stone bridge linking the Rue Joseph Kessel to the Rue de Tolbiac.
Conception: Bernard and Perouse.

Pont de Bercy (1864)

12th – 13th arrondissements.
Stone bridge linking the Boulevard de Bercy to the Boulevard Vincent Auriol.
Conception: Meunier, Monthioux, Savarin, Vaudrey and Warest.

Pont Charles-de-Gaulle (1996)

12th – 13th arrondissements
Steel bridge linking the Gare de Lyon and the Gare de Austerlitz, aligned with the Rue Van-Gogh.
Conception: Arretche and Karasinski.

Viaduct d'Austerlitz (1905)
12th – 13th arrondissements
Steel bridge linking the Gare
d'Austerlitz and Quai de la Rapée
metro stations on the n°5 line.
Conception: Bienvenue, Biette,
Briotet and Koechlin.

Pont d'Austerlitz (1855)
5th – 12th arrondissements.
Stone bridge linking the Place
Mazas and the Avenue Ledru-
Rollin, to the Place Valhubert and
the Boulevard Vincent-Auriol.
Conception: Choquet, Guiard,
Michal and Savarin.

Pont Sully (1877)
4th – 5th arrondissements.
Cast-iron bridge linking the
Boulevard Henri-IV to the
Boulevard Saint-Germain.
Conception: Brosselin and
Vaudrey.

Pont Marie (1630)
4th arrondissement.
Stone bridge linking the
Rue Nonnains-d'Hyères to the
Rue des Deux-Ponts.
Conception: Delagrange and
Marie.

Pont Louis-Philippe (1862)
4th arrondissement.
Stone bridge linking the Rue du
Pont-Louis-Philippe and the Rue
Joachim-du-Bellay.
Conception: Feline-Romany,
Garnuchot, Martin and Savarin.

Pont de la Tournelle (1928)
4th – 5th arrondissements.
Reinforced concrete bridge linking
the Rue des Deux-Ponts to the
Rue du Cardinal-Lemoine.
Conception: Deval, Lang, Retraint,
Pierre and Louis Guidetti.

Pont Saint-Louis (1970)
4th arrondissement.
Steel bridge linking the Île Saint-
Louis to the Île de la Cité.
Conception: Coste, Creuzot,
Jabouille and Long-Depaquit.

Pont d'Arcole (1854)
4th arrondissement.
Iron bridge linking the Place
l'Hôtel-de-Ville and the Rue
d'Arcole.
Conception: La Galisserie and
Oudry.

Pont Notre-Dame (1514)
4th arrondissement.
Stone and steel bridge linking
the Rue Saint-Martin to the
Rue de la Cité.
Conception: Aron, Binet, Drogue,
Résal and Rétraint.

Pont au Change (1860)
1st – 4th arrondissements.
Stone bridge linking the Place du
Châtelet to the Boulevard du
Palais.
Conception: Garnuchot, Vaudrey
and de La Galisserie.

Pont Neuf (1603)
1st – 6th arrondissements.
Stone bridge linking the Rue du
Pont-Neuf to the Rue Dauphine.
Conception: Cerceau,
Chambiges, Isles, Marchand and
Metezeau.

Pont de l'Archevêché (1827) 4th –
5th arrondissements.
Stone bridge linking the Quai de
l'Archevêché to the Rue des
Bernardins..
Conception: Plouard.

Pont au Double (1882)

4th – 5th arrondissements.
Cast iron bridge linking the Rue d'Arcole and the Rue Lagrange.
Conception: Bernard and Lax.

Petit Pont (1297)

4th – 5th arrondissements.
Stone bridge linking the Rue de la Cité to the Place du Petit-Pont and the Rue du Petit-Pont.
Conception: Darcel, de La Galisserie, Michal and Gariel.

Pont Saint-Michel (1387)

4th – 6th arrondissements.
Stone bridge linking the Boulevard du Palais to the Place Saint-Michel and the Boulevard Saint-Michel.
Conception: Vaudrey and de La Galisserie.

Pont des Arts (1984)

1st – 6th arrondissements.
Steel bridge linking the Quai du Louvre and the Place de l'Institut.
Conception: Arretche, De cessart and Dillon.

Pont du Carrousel (1939)

1st – 7th arrondissements.
Reinforced concrete bridge linking the Louvre to the Quai Voltaire.
Conception: Gaspard, Lang, Malet, Tourry and Umbdenstock.

Pont Royal (1632)

1st – 7th arrondissements.
Concrete bridge linking the Avenue du Général-Lemonnier to the Rue du Bac.
Conception: Gabriel, Hardouin-Mansart and Romain.

Passerelle de Solférino (2000)

1st – 7th arrondissements.
Steel bridge linking the Tuileries Gardens to the Rue de Solférino.
Conception: Mimram.

Pont de la Concorde (1792)

7th – 8th arrondissements.
Stone bridge linking the Place de la Concorde with the Quai d'Orsay and the Quai Anatole-France
Conception: Perronet and Prevost.

Pont Alexandre-III (1900)

7th – 8th arrondissements.
Steel bridge linking the Avenue Winston Churchill to the Esplanade des Invalides .
Conception: D'Alby, Cassien-Bernard, Cousin and Resal.

Pont des Invalides (1829)

7th – 8th arrondissements.
Stone bridge linking the Place du Canada to the Place de la Finlande.
Conception: Gariel, De La Galisserie, Savarin and Vaudrey.

Pont de l'Alma (1974)

7th – 8th arrondissements.
Steel bridge linking the Place de l'Alma to the Place de la Résistance.
Conception: Arsac, Blanc, Coste, Dougnac and Man Yick.

Passerelle Debilly(1900)

7th – 16th arrondissements.
Steel bridge linking the Avenue de New-York to the Quai Branly.
Conception: D'Alby, Lion and Resal.

Pont d'Iéna (1813)

7th – 16th arrondissements.
Stone bridge linking the Place de Varsovie and the Trocadéro Gardens to the Quai de Branly and the Champ de Mars.
Conception: Gaspart, Lamande and Morane.

Pont Bir-Hakeim (1906)

15th – 16th arrondissements.
Steel bridge linking the Rue de l'Albonie to the Place des Martyrs Juifs du Vélodrome d'Hiver and the Boulevard de Grenelle.
Conception: Biette, Formige and Thomas.

Pont Rouelle (1900)

15th – 16th arrondissements.
Iron bridge linking the Avenue du Président Kennedy to the Quai de Grenelle.
Conception: Bonnet, Moïse and Widmer.

Pont de Grenelle (1874)

15th – 16th arrondissements.
Steel bridge linking the Rue Maurice Bourdet to the Place Fernand Forest.
Conception: Chauvel, Creuzot, Grattesat, Jabouille, Pilon and Thenault.

Pont Mirabeau (1896)

15th – 16th arrondissements.
Steel bridge linking the Rue l'Amiral Cloué to the Rond-Point of the Pont Mirabeau.
Conception: D'Alby, Letellier, Rabel and Resal.

Pont du Gargliano (1966)

15th – 16th arrondissements.
Steel bridge linking the Boulevard Exelmans to the Boulevard Victor.
Conception: Davy and Thenault.

Pont Aval, called "Pont du Point du Jour" (1968)

15th – 16th arrondissements.
Concrete bridge allowing automobiles on the Périphérique to cross the Seine down river from Paris.
Conception: Arsene-Henry, Coste, Muzas, Pilon and Rousselin.

Not to forget:

The future Passerelle de la Bibliothèque (2005)

12th – 13th arrondissements.
Which will link the Bibliothèque de France to the Parc de Bercy.
Conception: Feichtinger.

BATEAUX MOUCHES

Bateaux Parisiens
Port de la Bourdonnais, 8th arr.
(+33) 1 44 11 33 44
www.bateauxparisiens.fr

Bateaux-Mouches

Pont de l'Alma, Right Bank, 8th arr.
(+33) 1 42 25 96 10
www.bateaux-mouches.fr

Bateau Vedettes de Paris

Port de Suffren, 7th arr.
(+33) 1 44 18 08 03
www.bateauxparisiens.fr

Bateaux Vedettes du Pont-Neuf

1, Square du Vert-Galant,
Île de la Cité, 1st arr.
(+33) 1 46 33 98 38
www.marinedebercy.com

Bateaux Parisiens

Port de la Bourdonnais, 8th arr.
(+33) 1 44 11 33 44
www.bateauxparisiens.fr

Batobus

Stops: Eiffel tower, Musée d'Orsay, Musée du Louvre, Hôtel de Ville, and Notre-Dame
(+33) 1 44 11 33 99
www.batobus.com

PASSAGES AND COVERED GALLERIES

Galerie Véro-Dodat
19, Rue Jean-Jacques-Rousseau
1st arrondissement.

Galerie Vivienne - Galerie Colbert

4, Rue des Petits-Champs
1st arrondissement.

Passage Choiseul
40, Rue des Petits-Champs
2nd arrondissement.

Passage du Grand-Cerf
146, Rue Saint-Denis
2nd arrondissement.

Passage Jouffroy
10, Boulevard Montmartre
2nd arrondissement.

Passage des Panoramas
10, Rue Saint-Marc
2nd arrondissement.

Passage des Princes
5, Boulevard des Italiens
2nd arrondissement.

Passage Verdeau
6, Rue de la Grande-Batelière
2nd arrondissement.

Passage Brady
33, Boulevard de Strasbourg
10th arrondissement.

**CONTEMPORARY PARKS
AND GARDENS**
Jardin des Halles (1986-1988)
Rue Berger
1st arrondissement.

Jardin de Cluny (2000)
Rue de Cluny
5th arrondissement.

Jardin du Bassin de l'Arsenal (1983)
Boulevard de la Bastille
12th arrondissement.
Parc de Bercy (1994-1997)
Rue Descos
12th arrondissement.

Square Charles-Péguy (1989)
Rue Rottembourg
12th arrondissement.

The Planted Path,
called "Coulée Verte" (1993)

Avenue Daumesnil
12th h arrondissement.

Jardin de Reuilly (1998)
Rue Montgallet
12th arrondissement.

Parc André-Citroën (1992)
Quai André-Citroën
15th arrondissement.

Jardin Atlantique (1994)
Place Raoul-Dautry
15th arrondissement.

Parc de la Turlure (1988)
Rue de la Bonne
18th arrondissement.

Square de la Place Stalingrad
(1990)
Place de Stalingrad
19th arrondissement.

Parc de la Villette (1987-1991)
Avenue Jean-Jaurès
19th arrondissement.

Parc de Belleville (1988)
Rue des Couronnes
20th arrondissement.

Jardin Sauvage Saint-Vincent
(1995)
Rue Saint-Vincent
20th arrondissement.

ZOOS
Ménagerie
Jardin des Plantes
57, Rue Cuvier
5th arrondissement.

Vincennes Zoo
53, Avenue de Saint-Maurice,
12th arrondissement.

CONTEMPORARY MONUMENTS
Forum des Halles
101 Porte Berger,
1st arrondissement.

Georges-Pompidou Center
Place Georges-Pompidou,
4th arrondissement.

Institut du Monde Arabe
1, Rue des Fossés-Saint-Bernard,
5th arrondissement.

Opéra-Bastille
Place de la Bastille,
12th arrondissement.

**Bibliothèque Nationale de France
- François Mitterand Site**
Quai François-Mauriac,
13th arrondissement.

**La Défense (THE C.N.I.T.
and the Grande Arche)**
Parc de la Défense, Neuilly.

MUST SEES
Palais-Royal
Rue de Valois
1st arrondissement

Place Vendôme
Rue de la Paix
1st arrondissement

Notre-Dame
Rue d'Arcole
4th arrondissement

Place des Vosges
Rue de Birague
4th arrondissement

Sainte-Chapelle
Boulevard du Palais,
4st arrondissement

Tour Saint-Jacques
Square de la Tour Saint-Jacques
4th arrondissement

Luxembourg Gardens
Boulevard Saint-Michel
6th arrondissement

The Eiffel Tower
Champs de Mars,
7th arrondissement

Hôtel des Invalides
Avenue du Mal Gallieni
7th arrondissement

Arc de Triomphe
Place Charles de Gaulle
8th arrondissement

Place de la Concorde
8th arrondissement

Opéra-Garnier
Place de l'Opéra,
9th arrondissement

Palais de Chaillot
Trocadéro
16th arrondissement

Sacré-Cœur
Place du Parvis du Sacré-Cœur
18th arrondissement

The Père-Lachaise Cemetery
Avenue Gambetta
19th arrondissement

Château de Versailles
Versailles 78000

VIRTUAL WALKS
www.paris-touristoffice.com
www.paris.fr
www.paris.org
www.ratp.fr
www.museums-of-paris.com
www.parisbalades.com
www.paris.culture.fr
www.capcite.com
www.myparisnet.com
www.visit-paris.com

Bibliography

Almanach des adresses des demoiselles de Paris de tout genre et de toutes les classes, 1792.

Christine Angot
Quitter la ville
© Éditions Stock, 2000.

Louis Aragon
Le Paysan de Paris
© Éditions Gallimard, 1919.

Paul Auster
Trilogie New Yorkaise,
La Chambre Dérobée.
© Actes Sud, 1988.

Walter Benjamin
Paris, Capitale du XIXe siècle
© Éditions du Cerf, 1989.

Juan Carlos Botero
Air France Magazine, 2001.

Édouard Boubat
Amoureux de Paris
1993, All rights reserved.

Claire Bretecher
Interview with Claude Servan-Schreiber, *Lire*, March 1977.

Jean-Paul Caracalla
Vagabondages Littéraires dans Paris
© Éditions de La Table Ronde, 2003.

Blaise Cendrars
Paris des Rêves, Éditions
Clairefontaine, 1950,
All rights reserved.

Maurice Chevalier
My Paris, 1972, All rights reserved.

Jean-Paul Clébert
Paris Insolite, Éditions Denoël, 1952.

Jean Cocteau
Journal 1942-1945
© Éditions Gallimard, 1989.

Jean Cocteau, *Opium.*
© Éditions Stock, 1930.

Honoré de Balzac
Les Illusions Perdues, 1838-1843.

Inés de la Fressange, Paris.
© Éditions Assouline, 2004.

Henry de Montherlant
© All rights reserved.

Bertrand Delanoë, Paris.
© Éditions Assouline, 2004.

Virginie Despentes, *Teen Spirit.*
© Éditions Grasset & Fasquelle, 2002.

Robert Doisneau
Trois Secondes d'Éternité. Éditions
Contrejour, 1979, All rights reserved.

Alain Ducasse, Paris.
© Éditions Assouline, 2004.

Jean Dutourd, preface to *Vingt ans avec Léon-Paul Fargue.*
© Éditions Mémoire du Livre, 1999.

Léon-Paul Fargue
Le Piéton de Paris
© Éditions Gallimard, 1939.

Jacques Garcia, Paris.
© Éditions Assouline, 2004.

Anna Gavalda
Je Voudrais que Quelqu'un m'Attende Quelque Part
© Éditions Le Dilettante, 1999.

Karen Elizabeth Gordon
Paris introuvable, Éditions
Abbeville, 1997, All rights reserved.

Julien Green, *Paris.*
© Librairie Arthème Fayard, 1995.

Sacha Guitry, *Si Paris nous Était Conté*, Presses de la Cité, 1993.

Bibliography

André Hardellet
Œuvre I, L'Arpenteur.
© Éditions Gallimard, 1990.

Ernest Hemingway
A Moveable Feast,
New York: Scribner. 1996.

Éric Holder
Nouvelles du Nord,
© Éditions Le Dilettante, 1984.

Michel Houellebecq
Les Particules Élémentaires,
© Éditions Flammarion, 1998.

Victor Hugo
Les Misérables, 1862.

Marcel Jouhandeau, *Un Monde*
© Éditions Gallimard, 1950.

Alphonse Karr, *Le Diable à Paris,
Paris et les Parisiens.* 1845.

Marc Lambron, *Carnet de bal,*
© Éditions Gallimard, 1992.

Jacques-Henri Lartique
L'Émerveillé, © Éditions Stock, 1981.

Le Corbusier, *La Ville Radieuse,*
© Fondation Le Corbusier.

Henry Miller, *Paris des rêves,*
Éditions Clairefontaine, 1950, droits
réservés.

Donald Grant Mitchell
*La France et les Français Vus
par les Voyageurs Américains,
1814-1848,* 1847.

Patrick Modiano
"La Seine", from *La Nouvelle
Revue Française,* 1981.

Paul Morand, *Paris.*
© La Bibliothèque des Arts, 1970.

Jacques Offenbach
La Vie Parisienne, 1866.

Georges Perec, *Perec/rinations.*
© Zulma, 1997.

Raymond Queneau, *Les Ziaux.*
© Éditions Gallimard, 1943.

Jules Renard, *Journal 1893-1898,*
1925.

Jules Romains, *Puissances
de Paris,* © Éditions Gallimard,
1919.

Sonia Rykiel, *Paris.*
© Éditions Assouline, 2004.

George Sand
*La Rêverie à Paris, Paris-Guide
par les Principaux Écrivains
et Artistes de la France,* 1867.

Alain Schifres, *Les Parisiens.*
© Éditions Jean-Claude Lattès,
1990.

François Simon, *Paris.*
© Éditions Assouline, 2004.

Stendhal, *Le Rouge et le Noir,*
1830.

Michel Tournier
© All rights reserved.

Zoé Valdés, *La Sous-Développée.*
© Actes Sud, 1996.

Index

a

b

d

e

f

j

k

l

m

s t

u

Index

Acknowledgements
&
Photographic Credits

All the photographs in this work were made by Max Dhéry with the exception of:
Pages 4-5, 50-51, 140, 156, 188, 291, 346-347, 364, 370-371, 384-385, 386-387, 388-389, 400-401, 402-403, 404 (top, right), 420-421, 432-433, 467, 501, 502-503, 544-545, 704, 705, 708-709, 710-711, 714-715, 730, 731, 735, 746, 759: © Photos Francesca Alongi et Fabrizio Veneziano.
Pages 38, 46, 52, 69, 72, 73, 76, 78, 82, 85, 86, 87, 92, 93, 112-113, 117, 118, 120, 121, 122, 123, 129, 130, 131, 133, 139, 141, 142, 144, 145, 154, 157, 166, 168, 170, 171, 174, 175, 176, 177, 178, 179, 182, 184, 185, 186-187, 189, 190, 194-195, 196, 197, 198, 199, 200, 201, 202, 204, 205, 206, 207, 209, 211, 212, 213, 216, 217, 220, 221, 224, 232, 233, 234, 237, 244-245, 249, 251, 252, 255, 257, 259, 260, 262-263, 264, 265, 266, 267, 268, 269, 270, 271, 272-273, 284, 285, 292, 294, 300-301, 302-303, 304-305, 323, 324, 325, 328, 329, 330, 332, 333, 335, 336, 338, 339, 357, 376, 377, 394, 408, 410-411, 416, 449, 450, 451, 457, 476, 477, 482, 484-485, 486, 516-517, 518, 519, 520-521, 522-523, 526-527, 530-531, 551, 552, 554, 568, 569, 572, 580, 584, 585, 586, 594, 606, 607, 608, 609, 610, 620, 621, 626-627, 632-633, 634-635, 642, 643, 644, 645, 652, 660, 661, 663, 690, 700, 707, 754, 761, 786, 794-795, 798, 806, 807, 813, 819, 862-863, 882, 883, 884-885, 897, 902, 903, 904, 905, 908, 911, 912, 920-921, 925: © Photos Assouline.
Pages 36-37: © RATP/Akimoff Licences.
Page 41: © Jean-Paul Goude.
Pages 46, 652, 705: Lighting of the Eiffel Tower © Société Nouvelle d'Exploitation de la Tour Eiffel/Conception Pierre Bideau/Photos Assouline (1,2), Francesca Alongi (3).
Page 69: © Pavillon des Antiquaires et des Beaux-Arts/Photo Assouline.
Pages 60, 110, 208-209, 240-241, 312-313, 592-593, 595, 651, 900-901: © Photo Daniel Aron.
Pages 72-73: Aristide Maillol, La Nuit, 1907-1909 © Adagp, Paris 2004/Photo Assouline.
Page 74: Aristide Maillol, L'Été, Flore, 1910 © Adagp, Paris 2004/Photo Max Dhéry.
Page 87: © Sculpture by Bernard Venet/Photo Assouline.
Pages 88-89, 94-95, 97, 100-101, 102-103, 104-105, 106-107, 148-149, 406-407, 508, 509, 564-565: © Photos Keiichi Tahara.
Pages 114-115: © Courtesy Le Cabaret.
Pages 180-181: Daniel Buren, Les Deux Plateaux, 1986 © Adagp, Paris 2004/Photo Max Dhéry.
Page 218: Place du Marché-Saint-Honoré, 1997 © Architecte Ricardo Bofill/Photo Max Dhéry.
Pages 225, 228, 229: © Photos Laziz Hamani.
Page 230: © Photo Jean-Louis Guillermin.
Page 236: © Photo Philippe Sebirot.
Page 251: Arman, L'Heure de tous, 1985 © Adagp, Paris 2004/Photo Assouline.
Pages 280-281, 286-287, 288-289, 296-297, 636, 797: © Photos Patrice Kezirian.
Pages 295, 676: © Photos Pamela Hanson.
Pages 352-353: Centre Georges-Pompidou, 1997 © Architects Renzo Piano and Richard Rogers/Photo Max Dhéry.
Pages 368-369, 526-527: © Photo Alain Perceval.
Page 375: © Commissariat Général au Tourisme/Fronval.
Pages 376, 377: Créations Prosper Assouline © Photos Assouline.
Page 380: © Photo Feuillie/All rights reserved.
Pages 400-401, 402-403, 405 : Institut du Monde Arabe, 1987 © Architects: J. Nouvel (principal architect), Architecture-Studio (M. Robain, R. Tisnado, J.-F. Bonne, J.-F. Galmiche) and G. Lezenes, P. Soria/Photos Francesca Alongi (1,2), Max Dhéry (3).
Page 461: © Photo Francastel/Rapho.
Page 466: César, Centaure, 1995 © Adagp, Paris 2004/Photo Assouline.
Page 501: Christine O'Laughlin, Les anges qui Passent, 1996-2004 © Photo Francesca Alongi.
Pages 526-527: © Photo Deidi Von Schaewen.
Pages 534-535: Eiffel Tower and detail of the Mur pour la Paix by Clara Halter and Jean Michel Wilmotte, 2000/Photo Max Dhéry.
Pages 548-549: © Photo Richard Aujard.
Pages 570-571: © Courtesy Spoon Food & Wine/Photo Joerg Lehmann.
Pages 574, 873: © Illustration René Gruau/www.rene-gruau.com.

Page 575: Illustration Karl Lagerfeld © Chanel/Karl Lagerfeld/Photo Assouline.
Pages 596-597: © Courtesy Crazy Horse/Photo Stéphane Cardinale.
Page 610: © Courtesy Artifort.
Pages 646-647: Maison Robert Mallet-Stevens, 1926 © Adagp, Paris 2004/Photo Max Dhéry.
Page 649: Villa La Roche-Jeanneret, Le Corbusier and Pierre Jeanneret, 1923 © FLC/Adagp, Paris 2004/Photo Max Dhéry.
Pages 688-689, 691, 692-693: Parc André Citroën © Architect Jean-Paul Viguier (with Alain Provost, landscape designer, Patrick Berger, architect, and Gilles Clément, landscape designer)/Photo Max Dhéry.
Pages 702-703, 704: Tour Montparnasse, 1973 © Architects Eugène Beaudoin, Urbain Cassan, Louis de Hoÿm de Marien and Jean Saubot/Photos Max Dhéry (1), Francesca Alongi (2).
Page 720: © Photo Angeli.
Pages 730, 731: Place de Séoul, 1985 © Architect Ricardo Bofill/Photo Francesca Alongi.
Page 748: Fondation Cartier pour l'Art contemporain, 1990-1994 © Architects J. Nouvel, E. Cattani & Associés, E. Cattani/Photo Max Dhéry.
Page 762-767: BNF, 1995 © Dominique Perrault Architect/Adagp, Paris 2004/Photo Max Dhéry.
Page 774: Ministère de l'Économie et des Finances, 1988 © Architects Paul Chemetov and Borja Huidobro/Photo Max Dhéry.
Pages 778-779: Palais Omnisports de Paris-Bercy, 1983 © Architectes Pierre Parat, Michel Andrault and Aydin Guvan/Photo Max Dhéry.
Page 782: Opéra National de Paris-Bastille, 1989 © Architect Carlos Ott/Photo Max Dhéry.
Pages 846, 848-849, 850-851, 854-855, 857, 858-859: La Villette, Cité des Sciences et de l'Industrie, La Géode, 1986 © Architect Adrien Fainsilber/Photo Max Dhéry.
Page 847: Grande Halle de la Villette © Restoration by Philippe Robert and Bernard Reichen/Photo Max Dhéry.
Pages 852, 853: La Villette, Cité de la Musique, 1990-1996 © Architect Christian de Portzamparc/Photo Max Dhéry.
Page 872: All rights reserved.
Pages 878-879: © Photo Sébastien Ratto-Viviani.

ACKNOWLEDGEMENTS

The editor would like to thank the artists and photographers who brought their generous contribution to this work: Akimoff, Arman, Eugène Beaudoin, Alexandre Bigle, Francesca Alongi and Fabrizio Veneziano, Daniel Aron, Richard Aujard, Ricardo Bofill, Daniel Buren, Paul Chemetov, Adrien Fainsilber, Jean-Paul Goude and Virginie Laguens, Jean-Louis Guillermin and Louise Bertaux, Clara Halter, Laziz Hamani, Pamela Hanson, Patrice Kezirian, Karl Lagerfeld, Clémence de Monpezat, Jean Nouvel, Christine O'Laughlin, Carlos Ott, Pierre Parat, Dominique Perrault, Renzo Piano, Christian de Portzamparc, Sébastien Ratto-Viviani, Richard Rogers, Keiichi Tahara, Bernar Venet, Jean-Paul Viguier, Deidi Von Schaewen and Jean Michel Wilmotte; the authors who agreed to participate: Christine Angot, Paul Auster, Juan Carlos Botero, Claire Brétecher, Jean-Paul Caracalla, Jean-Paul Clébert, Virginie Despentes, Jean Dutourd, Anna Gavalda, Karen Elizabeth Gordon, André Hardellet, Éric Holder, Michel Houellebecq, Marc Lambron, Patrick Modiano, Alain Schifres, Michel Tournier and Zoé Valdès; as well as the persons representing their rights: Danielle Adda Robert, Isabelle Alliel and Olivier Espaze, Nickie Athanassi, Martine Bertea, Annie Cognacq, Olivier Daulte, Stéphane Dieu, Laurent de Freitas Braganca, Laure Leroy, Franck Perrussel, Renaud Pisapia, Michel Richard, Fabienne Roussel and Barbara Porpaczy.
Finally, the editor would like to specially thank for their friendly collaboration: Jeremy Bellingard, Stéphane Busuttil, Ségolène Cazenave, Bertrand Delanoë, Alain Ducasse, Inès de la Fressange, Jacques Garcia, Priscille Neefs, Patrick Perrin, Sonia Rykiel, Régine, Axel Schmitt and François Simon.